300
UNSUNG WOMEN

D-L Nelson

BOOKS BY D-L NELSON

Fiction

Lexington: Anatomy of a Novel
Day Care Moms
Triple Decker
Murder in Edinburgh
Murder in Schwyz
Murder in Ely
Murder in Paris
Murder on Insel Poel
Murder in Geneva
Murder in Caleb's Landing
Running from the Puppet Master
Family Value
The Card
Chickpea Lover: Not a Cookbook

Non-Fiction

Coat Hangers and Knitting Needles
The Cockeyed Nipple

Donna-Lane NELSON
21-23 rue de la Liberté
66700 Argelès-sur-mer
France

First Edition 2024

Paperback ISBN 979-8-9903855-0-4
Kindle ISBN 979-8-9903855-1-1
ePUB ISBN 979-8-9903855-2-8

Cover Design by: Deirdre Wait

To Isabel Richard
Without you, this book would never have been written.

INTRODUCTION

In 1848 a group of women wrote a *Declaration of Sentiments* stating ". . . the history of mankind is a history of repeated injuries and usurpations on the part of man toward women, having in direct object the establishment of an absolute tyranny over her."

Throughout history, women have done amazing things against limitations of their gender. They've fought against the boundaries society has awarded to their hormones and still made contributions benefiting others.

Sometimes, they did get limited recognition, a building or a street named for them, an article in a newspaper, a write up in Wikipedia, Encyclopedia or book chronicling a certain discipline. Even a statue might be erected that people might or might not notice as they wander by.

Many of these women never became famous or have long been forgotten. Others are only known by a few within their areas of expertise. In too many cases, men were given credit for their accomplishments.

This book seeks to begin to correct this omission although it is only scratching the surface.

I've included revolutionaries who fought for their political beliefs that contrast to the most popular ideas in our day and age.

There are women who were effective even when I disagreed with their activities. Although there are more American women, I did not want only an American bubble perspective so women from other countries and beliefs are represented.

Some women were exceptional in the negative sense: witches,

pirates and serial killers, and they are included. These women went beyond the ordinary boundaries that define what the female sex SHOULD do.

Originally, I thought I would do it as a calendar, with a woman for each date, but on some days I had one woman and on others I had nine or more. I decided to list them by category. That way I didn't have to eliminate some very interesting women. That gave rise to another problem. Many of these women excelled in many different areas. Although I assigned them to their major successes, I listed other areas where they broke through the boundaries.

The hardest part was deciding who should be included. This book could be three or four times larger.

One of my biggest challenges was reducing these women's lives to between 100 and 200 words from 1,000+ words of research while preserving their essence. Capturing their lives in a limited number of words was like comparing the smell of a baking cake to a full pastry shop of cakes. In reality, most merit an entire biography and/or film about their lives.

Many women would have fit into several categories. For the biographies, I selected the one where I thought they cared the most or made the greatest contribution.

Research included delving into *Wikipedia*, articles, books, news and magazine articles and professional journals. Without the internet this book could not have been written.

I owe an incredible debt to friends who offered names: Julia Schmitz-Leuffen, Anne Hornung-Soukup and my husband Rick Adams among others. Without Isabel Richard, a friend from Geneva now living in Montréal, half the women listed wouldn't have been found.

I learned so much about these women with whom I would love to share a cup of tea like the inventor of the ironing board and dishwasher. I would love to talk with the feminists, the civil rights activists, the spies and revolutionaries. I want to ask the women who fought to be lawyers and doctors how they had the courage to keep going. As a non-sporty person, I so admire the mountain climbers, bicycle riders and parachute jumpers.

At the same time, I realized that so many of my gender having to fight so hard to fulfill their potential, hundreds of thousands of women were unable to break the bonds and humanity lost out on their talents.

This book is divided into three parts.

- Part 1 a list of women who made a contribution in a certain field. Each woman has a number.

- Part 2 The biographies of the women who made a contribution in a certain field.

- Part 3 Since the 300 women excelled in many areas, they are grouped by field for those readers that want to concentrate on a certain area or profession.

Readers may want to investigate these women further. I took inspiration from them. I hope you do too.

Part 1: This is a list of women with major accomplishments in certain categories. However, many of them made contributions in a number of fields.

ABOLITIONISTS
1. Lydia Maria Child
2. Lucretia Coffin Mott
3. Clarina Irene Howard Nichols
4. Sarah Parker Remond
5. Maria W. Stewart

ACADEMICS/SCHOLARS
6. Ada Sara Adler
7. Nora Kershaw Chadwick
8. Gertrude Mary Hirst
9. Janet Lembke

ACTIVISTS
10. Yelena Georgievna Bonner
11. Leyah (Leah) Chase
12. Crystal Catherine Eastman
13. Berta Isabel Caceras Flores
14. Nancy Green
15. Dorothy Irene Height
16. Maria Julia Hernandez
17. Jane Jacobs
18. Florynce Rae Kennedy
19. Muna Lee
20. Viola Fauver Liuzzo
21. Sarojini Naidu

40. Elisabeth Louise Vigée Le Brun
41. Shirley Ardell Mason
42. Maria Sibylla Merian
43. Elizabeth Catlett Mora
44. Rachel Ruysch
45. Augusta Christine Fells Savage
46. Miriam Schapiro
47. Amrita Sher-Gil
48. Elisabetta Sirani
49. Sophie Henriette Gertrud Taeuber-Arp

ASTRONOMERS

50. Williamina Fleming
51. Caroline Lucretia Herschel
52. Margaretha (Maria) Kirch
53. Henrietta Leavitt
54. Nicole-Reine Lepaute
55. Vera Florence Cooper Rubin
56. Beatrice Muriel Hill Tinsley

ATHLETES

57. Annie Cohen Kopchovsky
58. Marie Marvingt

ATOMIC BOMB VICTIM

59. Sadako Sasaki

AVIATION

60. Florence Lowe "Pancho" Barnes

CHILDREN'S ADVOCATE
83. Bertha Marian Holt

CONSERVATIONIST
84. Dian Fossey

COMPUTING EXPERTS
85. Anita Borg
86. Grace Brewster Hopper
87. Augusta Ada King
88. Arfa Abdul Karim Randhawa

CRIMINOLOGIST
89. Frances Glessner Lee

DANCER
90. Ayu Bulantrisna Djelantaik

ECONOMISTS
91. Sadie Tanner Mossel Alexander
92. Emily Greene Balch
93. Edith Abbott

EDUCATORS
94. Nannie Helen Burroughs
95. Dorothea Frances Canfield
96. Septima Poinsette Clark

ENGINEERS

ENVIRONMENTALISTS

FEMINISTS

121. Huda Sha'arawi or Hoda Sha'rawi
122. Kalliroe Parren

FILM / THEATER DIRECTORS
123. Vivica Aina Fanny Bandler
124. Larissa Shepitko

GEOGRAPHER
125. Ellen Churchill Semple

HISTORIANS
126. Bertha Eckstein-Diener
127. Mary Anne Everett Green
128. Ragnhild Hatton
129. Grace Raymond Hebard
130. Lucy Myers Wright Mitchell
131. Linda Nochlin
132. Etta Lubina Johanna Palm d'Aelders
133. Inayat Khan aka Nora Baker
134. Virginia Hall Goillot
135. Kitty Harris
136. Gabrielle Maria Petit
137. Agnes Smedley
138. Diana Ruth Wellesley

INVENTORS
139. Mary Elizabeth Anderson
140. Ruth Mary Rogan Benerito
141. Amalie Auguste Melitta Bentz

142. Josephine Cochrane
143. Caresse Crosby
144. Beulah Louise Henry
145. Margaret Eloise Knight
146. Elizabeth J. Magie Phillips

JOURNALISTS

147. Khadijah Muhammad Abdullah Al-Jahami
148. Louie Bennett
149. Marvel Jackson Cooke
150. Natalya Khusainovna Estemirova
151. Gauri Lankesh
152. Camille Lepage
153. Ella Maillart
154. Mary Margaret McBride
155. Georgette Louise Meyer (Dickey Chapelle)
156. Hazel Freeman Smith

LABOR LEADERS

157. Agnes Nestor
158. Marta Matamoros
159. Emma Anne Paterson
160. Crystal Lee Sutton

LAWYERS

161. Edith Hahn Beer
162. Marianne Beth
163. Margrith Bigler-Eggenberger
164. Bettisia Gozzadini
165. Lidia Poët

166. Clary Campoamor Rodriguez
167. Mary Ann Camberton Shadd Cary
168. Margaret Bush Wilson

LIBRARIAN
169. Pura Teresa Belpré y Nogueras

LINGUIST/TRANSLATOR
170. Lilias Eveline Armstrong
171. Kató Lomb

MAIL CARRIER
172. Mary Fields (Stagecoach Mary)

MARTIAL ARTS
173. Keiko Fukuda

MATHEMATICIANS
174. Marie-Sophie Germain
175. Elizabeth Lucar
176. Amalie Emmy Noether
177. Mary Somerville

MEDICAL DOCTORS
178. Safiye Ali
179. Kate Waller Barrett
180. Tewhida Ben Sheikh

181. Elizabeth Blackwell
182. Rebecca Lee Crumpler
183. Josefina Durocher
184. Marie Equi
185. Kate Campbell Hurd-Mead
186. Aletta Henriëtte Jacobs
187. Sophiea Louisa Jex-Blake
188. Mary Jane Safford-Blake
189. Clara Emilia Smitt-Dryselius

MIDWIVES

190. Marie-Anne Victoire Gillain Boivin
191. Angélique Marguerite Le Boursier du Coudray
192. Mary Carson Breckinridge
193. Marie-Louise Lachapelle

MILITARY

194. Lilian Bader
195. Pancha Carrasco
196. Susan Ahn Cuddy
197. Florence Beatrice Green
198. Mary Agnes Hallaren
199. Joy Bright Hancock
200. Sheila Anne Hellstrom
201. Kathleen Florence Lynn
202. Roza Georgiyevna Shanina
203. María Josefa Gabriela Cariño de Silang
204. Mary Anne Talbot (John Taylor)
205. Ecaterina Teodoroiu

MOUNTAIN CLIMBER
206. Wanda Rutkiewicz

NURSES
207. Sister Elizabeth Kenny
208. Baroness Eva Charlotta Lovisa Sofia (Sophie) Mannerheim
209. Gladys Skillett

PATHOLOGISTS
210. Sophia Getzowa
211. Alessandra Giliani

PHOTOGRAPHERS
212. Imogen Cunningham
213. Vivian Dorothy Maier
214. Lucia Moholy (Lucy Shultz)
215. Yevonde Philone Middleton (Professional name Madame Yevonde)

POLITICANS
216. Georgina Beyer
217. Anita Lee Blair
218. Hattie Ophelia Watt Caraway
219. Martha Wright Griffiths
220. Alexandra Mikhailovna Kollontai
221. Hazel McCallion
222. Maureen O'Carroll
223. Ana Pauker

RESISTANCE FIGHTERS
240. Jeanette Guyot
241. Irena Stanisława Sendler
242. Cecile Pearl Witherington Cornioley

REVOLUTIONARIES
243. Catherine Breshkovsky
244. Lil Milagro de la Esperanza Ramírez Huezo Córdoba
245. Haydée Santamaría Cuadrado
246. Mairéad Farrell
247. Vera Nikolayevna Figner Filippova
248. Heloise Ruth First
249. Vilma Lucila Espín Guillois
250. Fanny Efimovna Kaplan (Feiga Haimovna)
251. Musine Kokalari
252. Sybil (or Sibbell) Ludington
253. Constance Georgine Booth Markievicz
254. Marie-Jeanne 'Manon' Roland de la Platière
255. Pritilata Waddedar

SAILOR
256. Mary Ann Brown Patten

SCIENTISTS
257. Marian Ewurama Addy
258. Ana Aslan
259. Alice Augusta Ball
260. Alice Eastwood
261. Gertrude "Trudy" Belle Elion
262. Eloise "Elo" R. Giblett

263. Josephine Ettel Kablick
264. Kathleen Lonsdale
265. Ruth Sager
266. Maria Emilie Snethlage
267. Evelyn M. Witkin

SEAMSTRESSES

268. Ida Holdgreve
269. Esther Steinberg Gluck

SECRETARIES

270. Hermine "Miep" Gies

SLAVES

271. Harriet Jacobs
272. Bethany Veney

SOCIALISTS

273. Marina Ginestà i Coloma
274. Adelheid Dworschak Popps
275. Anna Strunsky Walling
276. Martha Beatrice Webb

SPORTS

277. Senda Berenson Abbott
278. Jill Kinmont Boothe
279. Emma Rowena Gatewood (Grandma Gatewood)
280. Lucy Walker

SUFFRAGISTS
281. Carrie Chapman Catt
282. Florence Hope Luscomb
283. Alva Erskine Belmont (Vanderbilt)

SURVIVORS
284. Eliza Gladys Dean aka Millvina Dean
285. Gisella Perl

TATTOO ARTIST
286. Maud Stevens Wagner

TERRORISM EXPERT
287. Eloise Randolph Page

TRANSGENDER
288. Lili Ilse Elvenes (Einar Wegener)

VETERINARIANS
289. Aleen Isobel Cust

WRITERS
290. Mary Anne Barker (Lady Broome, Lady Barker)
291. Minna Canth - Ulrika Wilhelmina Johnson
292. Elizabeth Gaskell
293. Mahasweta Devi
294. Nh Dini

295. Isabelle Wilhelmine Marie Eberhardt
296. Harriet Jane Farley
297. Ida A. Husted Harper
298. Irmgard Keun
299. Lucy Larcom
300. Catherine Lucille Moore

ABOLITIONISTS

Slavery was part of the formation of the United States of America. Blacks were considered 3/5ths of a person for a census count. The idea of one person owning another like a cow or a piece of furniture was repugnant to many women who threw themselves into the cause of freeing the slaves. Some fought the issue through their writings and public speaking while others offered their homes to runaway slaves as part of the Underground Railroad.

1. Lydia Maria Child

Born 11 February 1802 Medford, Massachusetts
Died 20 October 1880 Wayland, Massachusetts

Abolitionist
Native American Rights Activist
Journalist
Opponent of American Expansionism
Women's Rights Activist
Writer

"I was gravely warned by some of my female acquaintances that no woman could expect to be regarded as a lady after she had written a book," Child said. Considering she wrote other books including on subjects like abolition, Native American rights, black problems, household hints, frugality and any number of topics, her status as lady had to be in jeopardy. Her articles and books often shocked readers.

Child created *Juvenile Miscellany*, a monthly periodical for youngsters, with an emphasis on good morals.

She married journalist David Lee Child and together they worked on social justice issues, validating her idea men and women should and could work together.

Her novel *Hobomok* tells of an interracial marriage between an Indian and an American woman who had a son whom she wanted to integrate into white society. She published it anonymously. It was not well received.

When living in Wayland her home was part of the Underground Railroad housing runaway slaves.

2. Lucretia Coffin Mott
Born 3 January 1793 Nantucket, Massachusetts
Died 11 November 1880 Cheltenham, Pennsylvania of pneumonia

Abolitionist
Social Reformer
Women's Rights Activist

The discovery that male teachers were paid more than women teachers at the Nine Partners School where she had been a student then a teacher planted the seed of her interest in women's rights which grew into a forest.

She not only believed in abolition of slavery, she and her husband offered a stop on the Underground Railroad that provided safety for runaway slaves.

Her dedication to women's rights was strengthened when she and other women were excluded from the 1840 London Anti-Slavery Conference.

As an abolitionist, feminist, reformer and Quaker preacher she traveled around the country speaking for the causes she believed.

When the United States outlawed slavery in 1865, she advocated giving former slaves, both male and female, the right to vote.

She remained a central figure in reform movements until her death in 1880. The area around her long-time residence in Cheltenham Township is now known as La Mott, in her honor.

3. Clarina Irene Howard Nichols
Born 25 January 1810 Townshend, Vermont
Died 11 January 1885 Mendocino, California

Abolitionist
Farmer
Journalist
Lobbyist

Nichols was said to have knitted during important meetings. This didn't mean she was a quiet, housewifely kind of woman who did nothing for the causes she believed in: abolition, temperance, diet, dress reform and the women's movement.

Despite being raised in a well-to-do family she was energized by the hard times she faced. Her passions came from first-hand experience after a bad marriage which ended in divorce. Having to support her three children highlighted inequality in pay between men and women for her.

Her second marriage to a newspaper publisher gave her an outlet and a responsibility to take over for him when he was invalided.

She helped gather petitions to give women the vote which were submitted to the Vermont legislature in 1852.

Her anti-slavery activities included being part of the Underground Railroad, once even hiding an escaped slave in a cistern.

She moved to Kansas with her family to fight the 1854 Kansas-Nebraska Act to establish slavery there.

As a women's advocate, she became a speaker, giving the talk entitled *The Responsibilities of Women*.

4. Sarah Parker Remond
Born 6 June 1826 Salem, Massachusetts
Died 13 December 1894 Rome, Italy

Abolitionist
Activist
Lecturer

Remond was born a free woman in Massachusetts, but she encountered racism when she was not allowed to attend a private and later a public school. Her parents located a school that accepted African American children.

She was only 16 when she delivered her first anti-slavery speech, the first of many in the northeast United States and the United Kingdom.

One of her brothers, Charles Lenox Remond, often toured with her giving abolitionist lectures.

She worked with the American Anti-Slavery Society.

In 1858, Remond chose to travel to Britain to gather support for the growing abolitionist cause in the United States. While in London, Remond studied at Bedford College, lecturing during term breaks.

During the American Civil War, she appealed for support among the British public. After the conclusion of the war in favor of the Union, she appealed for funds to support the millions of the newly emancipated freed men in the American South.

5. Maria W. Stewart
Born c. 1803 Hartford, Connecticut
Died 17 December 1879 Washington, D.C.

Abolitionist
Domestic Worker
Lecturer
Women's Rights Activist
Writer

When she said (as a woman of color) that black men lacked "ambition and requisite courage" her followers were upset. As a result, her lecturing career ended seven months later.

She had been the first known woman to speak to a mixed gender and mixed racial audiences. Her topics were women's rights and slavery.

Orphaned at age three, she acted as an indentured servant for a minister and his family. After she moved to Boston, she continued working as a domestic.

When her husband died after three years of marriage, his executors cheated her out of any inheritance.

She lived with the family of David Walker of the General Colored Association. During this time, she wrote *Religion and the Pure Principles of Morality, The Sure Foundation on Which We Must Build* and *Meditations from the Pen of Mrs. Maria Stewart*.

After moving to Washington, D.C., she taught for 50 cents a month. White teachers earned double.

She was deeply religious.

ACADEMICS/SCHOLARS

Women once had to fight to attend a university. www.brookings.edu reports that 31% of full-time faculty posts are now held by women, a mere 5% increase in 75 years. Still harder for women is to qualify for tenure. The American Association of University Women reports that only 27% were fully tenured while the American Association of University Professors shows that the number of full-time university professors has increased since 1991. Women make up just 32.5% of full-time tenured or tenure-tracked professor. Their salaries are 81.2% of their male counterparts.

6. Ada Sara Adler
Born 18 February 1878 Copenhagen, Denmark
Died 28 September 1946 Frederiksberg, Denmark

Danish Classical Scholar

At a time when scholars were usually men, Ada Adler became a great woman philologist. Her work with classical languages, combing them with historical context, surpassed many men of her time.

Born into an exceptionally well-educated Jewish family, she had role models in her aunts who also broke educational barriers.

Adler studied at Copenhagen University. Her research included study on Pandora's myth.

Her work on a 10th century Byzantine encyclopedia of the ancient Mediterranean world called the *Suda* involved seeking out information from several countries.

The early years of her marriage to Anton Ludvig Christian Thomsen, Philosophy Professor at Copenhagen University, were intellectually supportive, but the couple eventually divorced.

Although she lectured at a university, she never achieved a regular appointment.

The Carlsberg Foundation provided her with financial support for assistants, travel, photographs and printing.

It took 16 years for her to produce Volume I of *Suda*.

In 1943 the Nazis deported all Danish Jews. While in Sweden she taught Greek to school children.

7. Nora Kershaw Chadwick
Born 28 January 1891 Lancashire, England
Died 24 April 1972 Cambridge, England

Academic
Philologist

Besides her work as a philologist, she and her husband, Cambridge professor Hector Munro Chadwick, ran literary salons.

Philology is the study of literary texts and oral and written records. The discipline goes back to the fourth century B.C.

Her main focus was on Celts research, and she also was a Lecturer in the Early History and Culture of the British Isles at Cambridge University.

Her work was recognized with honorary degrees from the Wales University, the National University of Ireland and St Andrews University.

She was made Commander of the Order of the British Empire in 1961.

She took an interdisciplinary approach when studying the cultures of the Anglo-Saxons, Celtics and Old Norse civilizations.

She translated sagas and ballads.

Collaborating with her husband she also produced three volumes about Eastern European languages.

8. Gertrude Mary Hirst
Born 22 January 1869 Huddersfield, England
Died 12 January 1962 Croton, New York

Classicist

As a classicist, Dr. Hirst published a claim in 1926 that Livy, a Roman historian, was born in 64 not 59 BC.

She came from a comfortable family with connections to a prime minister. Her siblings were successful as a journalist, an historian and a biographer.

She "read" (studied) classics at Cambridge before becoming a lecturer at Birmingham University.

She moved to the U.S. and taught at Louisville Female Seminary while continuing her studies at Columbia University where she earned a master's and a Ph.D.

The Journal of Hellenic Studies published her dissertation, *The Cults of Olbia*. From 1941 until her 1943 retirement, she was an assistant professor of Latin and Greek at Barnard College.

She did not follow conventions by living in a dormitory and was said to have ridden a bike down the middle of Broadway more than once.

9. Janet Lembke

Born 2 March 1933 Cleveland, Ohio
Died 3 September 2013 Staunton, Virginia

Author
Essayist
Naturalist
Translator
Scholar

Her life's work centered around classical Greek and Latin from Homer to Virgil. Besides her classical scholar credentials, she was a naturalist caring about the environment.

Her translations of Sophocles, Euripides and Aeschylus were published by Oxford University Press.

Her first book was *Bronze and Iron: Old Latin Poetry from Its Beginnings to 100 B.C.*

Novelist Annie Proulx wrote, "Lembke's writing tacks between three points: the stuff of her late-twentieth-century life; the tangle of creature and plant in every dimension of tide and river flow; and the haunting, connecting wires of mythos that still knot us to the ancient beginnings."

She was said to mix history, culture, personal anecdote, mythological allusion and poetic feeling.

ACTIVISTS

Activist is a broad term for women who were determined to improve the society where they lived. Middle- and upper-class women until the 20th century were considered too fragile to engage in men's activities. They were encouraged to be excellent housewives and mothers, but not to engage in any intellectual activities and certainly not in professions like doctors and lawyers. Lower-class women had little choice but to work, often in terrible conditions. Women, who saw societal injustices, were not expected to do anything about it, but many did, fighting to improve conditions for people. Almost all women in this book could be called activists, but the ones listed devoted themselves to a certain cause.

10. Yelena Georgievna Bonner
Born 15 February 1923 Merv, Turkmen SSR, Soviet Union
Died 18 June 2011 Boston, Massachusetts of heart failure

Activist
Physician

Bonner's husband Andrei Sakharov may have won the Nobel Prize for Peace, but his wife Yelana Bonner had her dissident credentials to match his. She survived surveillance, harassment, arrest and exile. She was said to have honesty and courage.

As early as the 1940s, Bonner had helped political prisoners and their families.

Her father had been executed during Stalin's purge and her

mother was sent to the Gulag for ten years.

She became a doctor and was a member of the Soviet Communist Party starting in 1964.

The crushing of the Prague Spring movement in 1968 convinced her that needed change could not come from within.

Bonner founded the Moscow Helsinki Group in 1976 and worked on behalf of Jews.

She fought to make her husband's writings available after his banishment to Gorky. She donated his papers to Harvard University.

She travelled frequently between the U.S. and Moscow.

Hers was the first signature on the "Putin Must Go" manifesto published online in 2010.

11. Leyah (Leah) Chase
Born 6 January 1923 Madisonville, Louisiana
Died 1 June 2019 New Orleans, Louisiana

Boxing Advisor
Civil Rights Activist
Chef

Leah Chase combined food and civil rights. Her New Orleans restaurant, Dooky Chase, featuring Creole cooking, was a 1960s meeting place for Civil Rights Movement strategy planners. Martin Luther King and his Freedom Riders used their rooms for meetings.

Local leaders were afraid to shut them down.

Registration drives were held there.

Chase was raised in poverty, relying on family-grown food: okra, peas, greens. Her multi-cultural roots were: African American, Spanish and French.

She moved from her small town to New Orleans to attend all black high school.

Overseeing nonprofessional boxers and working for a bookie were two of her early jobs, but she loved a third — waitressing.

Her husband was a jazz trumpeter, and his parents had a po-boy sandwich stand. The couple converted it to a sit-down restaurant.

The restaurant also promoted African American art. The restaurant in 2018 was listed as one of the 40 most important restaurants in U.S. by *Food &Wine*.

12. Crystal Catherine Eastman
Born 25 June 1881 Marlborough, Massachusetts
Died 28 July 1928 New York, New York of nephritis

Activist
Anti-militarist
Feminist
Journalist
Lawyer
Socialist

Eastman was a pioneer in that she kept her maiden name when she married her second husband and had a commuting marriage between London and New York. Her minister parents had raised her in an environment encouraging progressive causes.

After graduation from Vassar and Columbia University, she was second in her class from New York University Law School.

She fought for the right of women to vote, founded *The Liberator* magazine, co-founded the Women's International League for Peace (WILP), the Woman's Peace Party and Freedom and the American Civil Liberties Union (ACLU).

Working for *The Pittsburgh Survey*, she wrote *Work Accidents and the Law* which was used to fight for health and safety changes. She would draft a worker's compensation law.

Working with suffrage leaders like Alice Paul, she battled for women's right to vote. Unlike many suffrage proponents, she believed in the Equal Rights Amendment.

She took a stance against WWI and the Mexican War.

During the Red Scare of the early 1920s, she was blacklisted.

13. Berta Isabel Caceras Flores
Born 4 March 1971 La Esperanza, Honduras
Murdered 2 March 2016 La Esperanza, Honduras

Co-founder and coordinator of the Council of Popular and Indigenous Organizations of Honduras (COPINH)
Environmental Activist
Indigenous Leader

Warnings about her life being at risk were circulated for months before she was shot in the head. Three of the eight people linked to her death were U.S.-trained special forces at Fort Benning, Georgia.

She was from the Lenca people.

Her mother was a social activist, midwife, and mayor and was a role model for Cáceres who earned a teaching certificate.

At university she was an activist fighting logging and U.S. military bases on Lenca land.

When several world organizations planned to build four hydroelectric dams breaching international law and threatening the Lenca way of life and safety, Cáceres led protests. She took the case to the Inter-American Commission on Human Rights.

She was under threat after the 1989 Honduran coup with her name appearing with 17 others on a hit list.

One of her favorite sayings was, "They are afraid of us because we are not afraid of them."

14. Nancy Green
Born 4 March 1834 Mount Sterling, Kentucky
Died 30 August 1923 Chicago, Illinois in a car accident

Activist Civil Rights
Anti-Poverty Fighter
Civil Rights Fighter
Cook
Ex-slave
Icon
Nanny

Imagine being told you didn't exist as a person when millions know your face, although very few know your name. Green's picture appeared as Aunt Jemima on a pancake mix box.

She was born a slave. After the Civil War she lost her husband and lived in a shack.

A judge, whom she knew, suggested she become the symbol for the R.T. Davis Milling Company in Missouri.

She was 59 when her image was shown for the first tune on the world's largest flour barrel at a Chicago Expo.

Green became the company spokesman and for 20 years made personal appearances around the U.S. She would cook, sing and tell stories.

She used her status to rally against poverty and for equal rights.

When Quaker Oats was asked to support a monument for her grave, they replied that Aunt Jemina and Nancy Green weren't the same.

15. Dorothy Irene Height
Born 24 March 1912 Richmond, Virginia
Died 12 April 2010 Washington, D.C.

Rights Activist

Height's mantra was that civil rights and women's rights should be considered as a whole.

Although she was accepted at Barnard College, they had reached their 'two-negro quota' and banned her. She went on to earn degrees at New York and Columbia Universities.

She worked with the Harlem YWCA where Height helped integrate all YWCAs. There she met Mary McLeod Bethune, founder of the National Council of Negro Women (NCNW). Height would later be its president.

She was a tireless worker behind the scenes to organize the 1963 March on Washington. Despite working with Martin Luther King Jr., Philip Randolph, Roy Wilkins, Whitney Young, John Lewis and James Farmer, the "Big Six of the Civil Rights Movement" she was not invited to speak.

Working with Gloria Steinem, Betty Friedan and Shirley Chisholm, she helped found the National Women's Political Caucus.

16. Maria Julia Hernandez
Born 30 January 1939 San Francisco Morazán, Honduras
Died 30 March 2007 San Salvador, El Salvador of a heart attack

Human Rights Advocate

Hernández couldn't let El Salvador's 75,000 civil dead go unremembered. The war started in 1980 and lasted 12 years. A majority of the dead were peasants who never participated in the conflict.

The war was between left-wing guerillas such as the Farabundo Martí National Liberation Front and the army-backed Salvadoran government supported by the U.S. The United Nations has estimated that 85% of the atrocities were committed by government forces.

Without her drive in the mountains of eastern El Salvador, the bodies of murdered children still holding their toys would never have been found.

She founded and directed Tutela Legal, the human rights office of the Roman Catholic Archdiocese of San Salvador.

To accomplish her mission she spent her life, some 30 years, finding evidence of killings that became a book of the dead.

She never married and lived frugally in a single room.

17. Jane Jacobs
Born 4 May 1916 Scranton, Pennsylvania
Died 25 April 2006 Toronto, Canada

Activist
Theorist
Writer

Jacobs's work in urban studies was often disparaged by her male colleagues. It did not help that she had no formal university credentials despite studying at Columbia University's School of General Studies for two years and taking a wide variety of subjects. She was also suspected of being a Communist, which she was not.

Her theory expressed in *The Death and Life of Great American Cities* (1961) and her other six books and articles advanced her ideas that urban renewal and slum clearance disrespected city-dwellers. She countered opposition to her theories with grassroot efforts to protect neighborhoods.

She helped the cancellation of the Lower Manhattan Expressway. So vocal, she was arrested. She did the same thing in Toronto when opposing the Spadina Expressway.

Her view was that cities were living ecosystems that required bottom-up community planning from people who lived there because they knew what was best.

She wrote for many magazines such as *Fortune* and *Architectural Forum*.

18. Florynce Rae Kennedy
Born 11 February 1916 Kansas City, Missouri
Died 21 December 2000 New York, New York

Activist
Actress
Lecturer

Kennedy was flamboyant, often wearing a cowboy hat, pink sunglasses and false eyelashes which she called "Daffy Duck Lashes."

Despite majoring in pre-law at Columbia University, she was denied admission to its law school and was told it was because she was a woman, not because she was black. When she threatened to sue, they reversed their decision.

As a lawyer she represented some big names like Billie Holliday and Charlie Parker.

She acted in films, TV and worked as a narrator.

Her activism included a boycott of Coca-Cola to encourage the company to hire black drivers. They caved.

Her Media Workshop created strategies to encourage media to hire more blacks.

She said, ". . . niggerizing techniques that are used don't only damage black people, but they also damage women, gay people, exprison inmates, prostitutes, children, old people, handicapped people, native Americans. And that if we can begin to analyze the pathology of oppression… we would learn a lot about how to deal with it."

19. Muna Lee
Born 29 January 1895 Raymond, Mississippi
Died 3 April 1965 San Juan, Puerto Rico from lung cancer

Activist
Feminist
Poet
Teacher
Translator

Lee taught in Oklahoma and Texas, but like many writers wrote around her job responsibilities.

In 1916, she was first published in *Poetry*, a literary magazine.

She moved to New York, taught herself Spanish and worked as a translator for the U.S. Secret Service during World I.

A long-term resident of Puerto Rico from 1920 to her death 45 years later, she was an activist in the 1920s and 1930s, working on issues of women's suffrage and equal rights in Puerto Rico and Latin America.

Lee worked for more than two decades in cultural affairs for the United States State Department, promoting artistic and literature exchanges between Latin America and the U.S., as well as other countries.

Her marriage to Luis Munoz Marin, a poet and future first governor of Puerto Rico, ended in divorce.

Lee translated Spanish poetry, wrote her own and a novel.

20. Viola Fauver Liuzzo

Born 11 April 1925 California, Pennsylvania
Assassinated 25 March 1965 of Selma, Alabama of gunshot wounds

Civil Rights Activist

The Ku Klux Klan shot and killed Liuzzo as she was driving activists to the Montgomery airport. There were three people in the car, one was an FBI informant. Alabama did not convict the men, but the Federal government did. The FBI informant went into the witness protection program.

Her family was poor. Her activism was motivated by what she saw of the tensions between the races when the family moved to Ypsilanti, Michigan. Because her family moved often, her education was interrupted, but she did study at Wayne State University.

Liuzzo was an active supporter of Martin Luther King and marched across the Edmund Pettus Bridge. She helped with the logistics of the march.

She was married three times and had five children.

21. Sarojini Naidu

Born 13 February 1879 Hyderabad, Hyderabad State, British Raj
Died 2 March 1949 Lucknow, United Provinces, Dominion of India of cardiac arrest

Activist
Poet
Politician

She proved Mahatma Ghandi wrong after he said he didn't think women would be strong enough for a protest. Called the Nightingale of India for her poetry, she was also a fighter for civil rights, women's emancipation and Indian independence.

Like Mahatma Ghandi she believed in non-violence.

Naidu went to London in 1919 as a part of the British rule All India Home Rule League to advocate for freedom from the British Empire.

She married a doctor.

She accepted the Indian National Congress presidency in 1925. She became the first woman Governor in the Dominion of India.

Naidu's poetry includes both children's poems and others written on more serious themes including patriotism and tragedy. Published in 1912, *In the Bazaars of Hyderabad* remains one of her most popular poems.

Her talks on independence and women's rights were well received. She included poetry in some of her talks.

22. Mary White Ovington
Born 11 April 1865 Brooklyn, New York
Died 15 July 1951 Newton Highlands, Massachusetts

Activist
Journalist
Socialist
Suffragist
Writer

Like her parents, Ovington was active in women's rights and African American issues.

Listening to Frederick Douglas and Booker T. Washington in 1890 fired her interest in civil rights.

When she delivered Christmas presents to Ida B. Wells's family, she was upset by their living conditions. She began her fight with New York City to update tenements. She and Wells became friends and co-founded the National Association for the Advancement of Colored People (NAACP).

This led to her becoming involved in other issues such as employment.

She gave speeches at 14 colleges encouraging better race relations.

She became a socialist and met with Niagara Movement members who opposed segregation.

The group called a meeting that led to the formation of the NAACP. For 38 years, Ovington was part of the first NAACP office staff while remaining active in the campaign for women's voting rights.

She wrote for various papers and magazines on social issues and authored books about African American issues.

23. Conception Arnel Ponte
Born 31 January 1820 Ferrol, Spain
Died 4 February 1893 Vigo, Spain of chronic bronchitis

Activist
Feminist
Journalist
Lawyer
Poet

As the first woman to attend a Spanish University, she was forced to wear men's clothing.

During her life she would embrace many different roles.

She received her law degree in 1848 then married a lawyer and writer. The couple collaborated on a liberal newspaper until his death.

She founded two organizations: Saint Vincent de Paul, a feminist group, and Construction Beneficiary for worker housing.

During the Carlist War, she worked in a hospital with the Red Cross and later was its Secretary General.

Her interest in prisoners was strengthened by her serving as Inspector of Women's Correctional Houses.

A fighter for women, prisoners and other marginalized people, her work was recognized by the Academy of Moral Sciences and Philosophy, the first woman to be so honored.

She fought the concept that women were inferior and wrote many topics about women's education, the death penalty and related social issues.

Health issues plagued her all her life.

24. Annie Mae Aquash Pitou (Mi'kmaq name Naguset Eask)
Born 27 March 1945 Shubenacadie, Nova Scotia
Murdered mid-December 1975 Pine Ridge Reservation, South Dakota by bullet

Activist First Nations

Some thought this Indigenous activist to be an FBI informant, which may have led to her murder.

As part of the American Indian Movement (AIM), she participated in major occupations and demonstrations: Wounded Knee and Trail of Broken Treaties, Anicinabe Park and the Department of Interior.

Her focus was on education and resistance to police brutality against First Nations people.

Pitou was born on the Indian Brook Reserve and raised in poverty. She had tuberculosis at age eight.

Her family moved to Boston where she joined other urban Indians.

Geographically she was active in Minneapolis, Kenora, Ontario and Pine Ridge Reservation.

She worked on the Teaching and Research in Bicultural Education School Project (TRIBES), whose goal was teaching young Indians their history.

She and other Indian activists were arrested when police pulled over an RV, donated by Marlon Brando. Ten days later she was released.

She disappeared in December 1975. Her body was found the following February.

25. Ernestine Louise Polowsky Rose

Born 13 January 1810 Piotrków, Trybunalski, Warsaw, Poland
Died 4 August 1892 Brighton, England

Abolitionist
Feminist
Freethinker
Suffragist

Some reactions to Rose were that she should be tarred and feathered and that she was worse than a prostitute.

Called the first Jewish feminist, suffragist, abolitionist, and freethinker, Rose is almost forgotten in contemporary discussions of the American women's rights movement. However, she was a major intellectual force in the nineteenth century.

She claimed that she had become a rebel at five telling her rabbi father how she questioned a god who demanded hardships.

She went to court to stop the marriage her father had arranged.

To fund her travels, she invented and sold perfumed paper.

When sailing to England, she was shipwrecked, leaving her destitute.

Well known on a liberal speaker's circuit, she and Robert Owen founded the Association of All Classes of All Nations, a group promoting human rights for all people of all nations, sexes, races, and classes. After moving to New York, she continued to speak on abolition, equality for women, religious tolerance and slavery. She wrote the first petition for women's property rights.

26. Doris Gwendolyn Tate
Born 16 January 1924 Houston, Texas
Died 10 July 1992 Los Angeles, California of brain cancer

Activist

People know more about her daughter, Sharon, killed by the Manson family, than they do about Doris Tate.

After her daughter's slaughter, Tate fell into a depression until she decided to help change California laws for victims of violent crimes.

She joined groups: Parents of Murdered Children, Victim Offender Reconciliation and Justice for Homicide Victims groups. She founded COVER, the Coalition on Victim's Equal Rights, and served as a victims' representative on the California State Advisory Committee on Correctional Services.

She was part of a group that worked toward the passage of Proposition 8, the Victim's Rights Bill, allowing for victim impact statements prior to sentencing.

Her daughter's killers deserved the death penalty, she believed.

When one of the murderers was up for parole, she gathered 350,000 signatures to stop it.

George H.W. Bush recognized her contributions in 1992 at a Thousand Points of Light ceremony.

27. Zitkala-Sa (Red Bird) Simmons Bonnin
Born 22 February 1876 Yankton Indian Reservation,
Dakota Territory
Died 26 January 1938 Washington, D.C.

Activist
Educator
Editor

Musician
Translator
Writer

Living in two cultures is enriching and/or difficult. Zitkala-Ša wrote several works chronicling her struggles with cultural identity, and the pull between the majority culture in which she was educated and the Dakota culture in which she was raised.

Her books were among the first works to bring traditional Native American stories to a widespread white English-speaking readership.

Working with musician William F. Hanson, Zitkala-Ša wrote the libretto and songs for *The Sun Dance Opera* (1913), the first American Indian opera. It was composed in romantic musical style and based on Sioux and Ute cultural themes.

She was co-founder of the National Council of American Indians in 1926, which was established to lobby for Native peoples' right to United States citizenship and other civil rights they had long been denied. She could have been listed under several categories, but all her work helped spread information about American Indian culture and problems.

ACTRESS

During Roman times, actors, men and women were most often slaves. In Shakespeare's day, women's roles on stage were played by men. Most early English drama plays were a variation of Bible stories. Eventually women were allowed on stage, but they were often thought of as prostitutes. Actresses Nell Gwynn and Moll Davis were two actresses that were the mistresses of the king.

28. Jean Muir (Fullarton)
Born 13 February 1911 Suffern, New York
Died 23 July 1996 Mesa, Arizona

Actress
Educator
Labor Leader

Muir was the first blacklisted performer during the Joseph McCarthy Era. Her name was listed in *Red Channels*, a right-wing journal listing 151 performers said to be manipulating the entertainment industry with pro-Communist ideas.

After her name appeared she was dropped from the television program she was making in the role of Mrs. Aldrich. The sponsor was General Foods.

Although she lost the role of Melanie in *Gone with Wind*, she did appear in 14 films.

Studio executives disliked her for her part in the founding of the Screen Actors Guild.

For six months she had been a member of the Congress of American Women, a progressive group termed subversive. "I am not a Communist, have never been one, and believe that the Communists represent a vicious and destructive force," she said.

She became the Master Acting Teacher at Stephens College, completing a degree at the same time. She later headed the drama department at University of Missouri–Kansas City.

ANTHROPOLOGISTS

Feminist anthropology came into its own in the 1970s, focusing on the archeological, biological, cultural and linguistic. Many women who wrote about anthropology were wives of anthropologists in the field. An early definition in Denmark in 1674: "Anthropology, that is to say the science that treats of man, is divided ordinarily and with reason into Anatomy, which considers the body and the parts, and Psychology, which speaks of the soul." Today it is more the study of human behavior within a culture.

29. Ila Cara Deloria Anpetu Waste Win (Beautiful Day Woman)
Born 31 January 1889 Yankton Indian Reservation, South Dakota
Died 12 February 1971 of pneumonia

Anthropologist
Educator
Ethnographer
Linguist
Writer

Delora was a Yankton Dakota (Sioux), raised and educated on a reservation. Her father was an Episcopalian priest. Her mother was a U.S. Army general's daughter.

She was multilingual (English, Lakota, Dakota, Nakota and Latin) and bicultural.

Educated at Oberlin College and Columbia University, she won the respect of anthropologist Franz Boas as "one of the first truly bilingual, bicultural figures in American anthropology, and an extraordinary scholar, teacher, and spirit who pursued her own work and commitments under notoriously adverse conditions." Working with Boaz, she concentrated on native American language linguistics. She would challenge him and other white male anthropologists on cultural differences.

Her research was helped by her language skills, including in-depth first-hand experiences of Indian life.

Her life had financial difficulties. Once she lived in her car to afford to continue her research.

She died before finishing a Lakota-English dictionary.

30. Zora Neale Hurston
Born 7 January 1891 Notasulga, Alabama
Died 28 January 1960 Fort Pierce, Florida of heart disease

Anthropologist
Educator
Filmmaker
Harlem Renaissance Influencer
Maid
Writer

Writer Alice Walker was responsible for a renewal of interest in Hurston's work when she wrote an article in *Ms.*; Hurston had fallen into obscurity. She produced short stories, plays, essays and four novels.

Today she is better known for her writing than her anthropological and ethnographic research.

The granddaughter of four former slaves and the daughter of a minister and mayor of her town, she was one of eight children.

The introduction to reading was by a teacher who gave her books.

Hurston considered that her "birth."

Charlotte Osgood Mason, a philanthropist, helped finance her research.

In Harlem she met poet/playwright Langston Hughes.

Caring about Negro expression, she established a dramatic arts school at Bethune-Cookman College. Her own research reflected her dedication to the black experience on many artistic levels.

Her papers were saved from burning when a friend passed her house as a yardman was destroying them. They were given to Florida University library.

ARCHEOLOGISTS/ PALEONTOLOGISTS

Archeology as a formal study began in the 19th century. In the beginning women were discouraged from participating, although in the 1870s some universities allowed women to study the subject. Often it was the wealthy that did the investigations. Women's roles advanced through the 20th but often the women were married to the archeologist. Many worked as conservators and report writers.

31. Elizabeth Grayson Hartley FSA
Born 1947 Summit, New Jersey
Died 31 January 2018 York, England

Archeologist
Curator

Hartley spent most of her career as the Keeper of Archeology at the Yorkshire Museum in York (1971-2007). Peter Addyman, Director of the York Archeological Trust, described her as the "most determined, imaginative and devoted American expert – whose legacy to her adopted city will extend far into the future."

Her education included Mount Holyoke College, Edinburgh University and London University.

Her books include:
- *The Vikings in England,* winner of the European Museum of the Year Special Exhibition Award
- *Alcuin & Charlemagne: The Golden Age of York*

• *Constantine the Great: York's Roman Emperor*

When the nearby Malton museum, where she was a trustee, was moving, she arranged an exhibition for them.

32. Mary Douglas Leakey
Born 6 February 1913 London, England
Died 9 December 1996 Nairobi, Kenya

Paleoanthropologist

When she was a child the Douglas family traveled extensively in Egypt, Italy, France and the U.S., which developed Leakey's fascination of paleoanthropology.

Despite her professional success as an adult, she boasted of only failing examinations in the Catholic convent school which she attended. She was expelled from two schools, one for not co-operating in reciting poetry and once for a chemistry lab explosion. Her lack of grades made university admission impossible.

Her first dig was at 17 where she illustrated finds.

She and Louis Leakey, another paleoanthropologist, met when she worked with him as an illustrator. They married in 1936. Although the couple often worked as a team on excavations, credit often went to him.

After her husband's death she became director of excavations at Olduvai.

To keep the family's traditions alive, she trained her son in the field.

33. Lady Hester Lucy Stanhope
Born 12 March 1776 Chevening, England
Died destitute 23 June 1839 Lebanon in her sleep

Adventurer
Antiquarian
Archeologist
Aristocrat

Sometimes known as Queen Hester, she was considered the first Biblical archaeologist for her work in Palestine.

She was also one of the first to use any text, a medieval Italian text, in the planning. She also tried new methods that would become the norm.

Most members of the British aristocracy were not the adventurer and traveler that Queen Hester was.

As a child she lived with her grandmother until she moved to her uncle's home. He was the British statesman William Pitt, the Younger. There she acted as his hostess, the more traditional role for a woman of her class and time.

Although she had a pension, she used it to pay Syrian debts, dying penniless.

34. Gertrude Caton Thompson
Born 1 February 1888 London, England
Died 18 April 1985 Hereford, England

Archeologist

From bottle washer at a French excavation in 1915 to being the target of hate mail for her theory on native civilizations in Zimbabwe, Thompson dedicated her life to archeology. She filed the hate mail under the word "insane."

The seed for her interest in archeology was planted during a 1911 Egyptian trip with her mother.

The threat of cobras and hyenas nearby did not stop her from sleeping in a tomb at one dig.

She was acclaimed for her techniques in excavations.

She worked with the Prehistoric Society and the Royal Anthropological Institute.

Because of a 1912 inheritance, she never needed to worry about financing.

Meticulous in her systematic organization and recording of sites, she was the first to use air surveillance to locate potential archaeological sites.

For work in Zimbabwe, she organized an all-woman team.

ARCHITECTS

The National Architectural Accrediting Board (NAAB) annual report stated in the 2017-18 academic year archeology 48% of the 5,995 accredited architecture degrees were awarded to women. The degree is a requirement for an architectural license. However, in associate programs only 25% were women for the same period. The Bureau of Labor Statistics (BLS) said that in 2019 out of 208,000 architects only 25% were women. The National Council of Architectural Registration Boards (NCARB) said in 2022 there were 121,603 licensed U.S. architects, but only 2% are black.

35. Julia Morgan
Born 20 January 1872 San Francisco, California
Died 2 February 1957 San Francisco, California

Architect
Engineer

Morgan (nickname J.M.) had many powerful influences in her life, including her wealthy mother and grandmother. While living in New York near her grandparents, she met architect Pierre Le Brun, who encouraged her education.

As a student at the University of California, Berkley when women were not allowed to use the gymnasium, she helped found a chapter of the YWCA, thus lifting the restriction. She graduated in 1894 with a B.S. in engineering, the first woman to do so.

It took her three tries to be accepted at the *École Nationale Supérieure des Beaux-Arts* in Paris after the school succumbed to pressure to admit women.

Back in California she worked for an architect, who reportedly said that she was "an excellent draftsman whom I have to pay almost nothing, as it is a woman."

She opened her first office in her home, which burned during the 1906 earthquake and a second in an office building.

She received many commissions designing 700 buildings in California. The most famous was Hearst Castle. Despite her many impressive works, she flew under the radar.

36. Norma Merrick Sklarek
Born 15 April 1926 Harlem, New York
Died 6 February 2012 Los Angeles, California

Architect
Teacher

As the daughter of Trinidad immigrants, Sklarek became the first African American woman to become a licensed architect in two states: New York and California.

As a good student in mathematics and visual arts, her doctor father encouraged her to study architecture.

She was the only African American woman to receive a Bachelor of Architecture from Columbia University.

Nineteen architectural firms rejected her before Skidmore, Owings & Merrill hired her.

She taught architecture at New York City College.

Gruen and Associates made her their first female vice president.

She later moved to Los Angeles and was promoted to director. The males in the firm were often listed as design architect while she was called project architect.

Because she wanted to work on large projects, she found a home with the Jon Jerde Partnership.

Among her major projects was the U.S. Embassy in Tokyo.

She chaired the American Institute of Architects National Ethics Council.

ARTISTS

For this grouping I have defined artists as painters, designers, sculptors, people who create images in materials. If each women artist had a book written about her, it would fill a library, but few make international and multi-century recognition.

37. Gillian Ayres
Born 3 February 1930 London, England
Died 11 April 2018 North Devon, England of a heart attack and pancreatitis

Artist
Educator
Printmaker

Ayres received a progressive education based on the principles of Frederich Fröbel, which emphasized the recognition of each child's unique capabilities. She was said to be obsessed with painting from age 13.

She once said that her paintings were like "ice cream, cakes, seaweed, shells and hats!" She titled her paintings often only after completion.

She co-taught art to children in bomb-damaged parts of London and then made the decision to go to the Camberwell School of Art (1946-1950).

She was the first woman to run a British art school department at the Winchester School of Art. She taught until 1981 when she moved to Wales to devote herself full-time to painting.

One of her projects at the South Hampstead High School London was covered with wallpaper. Fortunately, when the wallpaper was removed, the project was not destroyed.

She was also a printmaker.

38. Maria Martin Bachman
Born 3 July 1796 Charleston, South Carolina
Died 27 December 1863 Columbia, South Carolina

Painter

When John James Audubon was creating his books, *The Birds of America* and *Viviparous Quadrupeds of North America*, he had three assistants. Only one was a woman, Bachman, who created many of the backgrounds. Most of her work was in watercolors.

She was prepared for the work after several field trips with her brother John, where she learned the techniques. He expressed his admiration for his sister's work when he wrote to Audubon, saying that she "knocks to the right and left with your articles and mine-- lops off, corrects, criticizes, abuses and praises by turn ... and... she does wonders."

Her personal life included caring for his sister's family until her death. Bachman later married her brother-in-law.

The hairy woodpecker (*Picus martinae*) was named after Martin by Audubon.

39. Ruth Windmüller Duckworth
Born 10 April 1919 Hamburg, Germany
Died 18 October 2009 Chicago, Illinois

Artist

Sculptor

Duckworth started drawing when she was homebound as a child, based on a doctor's recommendation. Her brother, who was going to watch over her, died when a Japanese submarine hit the ship he was on.

As a Jew, she was forbidden to study art in Germany. In 1936 she moved to England to attend the Liverpool School of Art and later at the Hammersmith School of Art and The City and Guilds of London Art School.

She felt she could study sculpting, drawing and painting rather than focus on just one, citing that Michelangelo had done just that.

In 1949 after her marriage the couple moved to the United States where she taught at Chicago University. Most of her work is with ceramics, bronze, porcelain and stoneware.

40. Elisabeth Louise Vigée Le Brun
Born 16 April 1755 Paris, France
Died 30 March 1842 Paris, France

Artist

A portrait of Marie Antoinette, one of the 30 LeBrun painted of the queen, caused a scandal because the queen was in simple dress. The artist repainted it. She was the subject of other scandals including love affairs with high-ranking people. Painting her daughter with her mouth open created yet another controversy.

When she wanted one of her portraits back, the subject refused, hiding the work under his bed. Le Brun had it "stolen."

She was a successful portrait painter before age 20, but her studio was closed because she lacked a license.

She married Charles LeBrun partially to get away from her

stepfather. The marriage was kept secret because he was engaged to another woman.

The *Académie Royale de Peinture et de Sculpture* made her a member, one of only 15 women accepted between 1648 and 1793.

She fled the French Revolution.

Her output included 660 portraits and 200 landscapes.

41. Shirley Ardell Mason

Born 25 January 1923 Dodge City, Minnesota
Died 26 February 1998 Lexington, Kentucky of breast cancer

Artist
Sufferer of Multiple Personality Disorder

Mason was the real Sybil, the book about a woman with 16 distinct personalities written by Flora Schreiber. There have been questions about the veracity of her case.

An artist, she studied at Minnesota State University Mankato and Columbia University.

Although she suffered from emotional breakdowns and headaches, she worked as a substitute teacher and had a home art gallery.

She sought psychiatric help from Cornelia Wilbur, who discovered Mason's multiple personalities. When Wilbur developed Parkinson's, Mason moved in to help care for her.

A second psychiatrist, Herbert Spiegel, had his doubts about Wilbur's diagnosis, thinking she had manipulated Mason. Debbie Nathan, author of *Sybil Exposed*, advances the theory that the cause of her problems was being raised by an abusive mother.

After her death some 100 paintings were found, some signed, some not. The unsigned are thought by some to be the work of alternative personalities.

42. Maria Sibylla Merian
Born 2 April 1647 Frankfort, Germany
Died 13 January 1717 Amsterdam, Netherlands

Artist
Naturalist
Scientific illustrator

Merian, as an adolescent, had an unusual hobby for a girl. She collected insects. At 13 she raised silkworms. She is considered one of the first European naturalists to observe and document insects. Some called her the David Attenborough of entomology.

Her training came from her stepfather, Jacob Marrel. By 1679, Merian had accumulated enough work to publish a book with 50 plate engravings of caterpillars.

During her lifetime she traveled to other countries to continue her work.

When she moved to Nuremberg with her husband, she painted and created embroidery designs. She gave art lessons to children of wealthy parents and published flower pattern books.

Merian, her mother and daughters moved to a stately home that was part of the Labadist community of about 60 religious people at the time. She studied natural history and Latin there.

When she later moved to Amsterdam, she earned her living by selling her paintings and opening a shop to sell her work.

43. Elizabeth Catlett Mora
Born 15 April 1915 Washington, D.C.
Died 2 April 2012 Cuernavaca, Mexico

Sculptor
Teacher

Mora, who graduated from Howard University cum laude, was another negro woman accepted at a school and then not admitted when the institution discovered she was black. That school was the Carnegie Institute of Technology.

Finding it hard to earn a living as an artist, Mora often turned to teaching. Eventually her works were selling for $10,000.

When she received a 1946 fellowship, she began a 20-year stay and became head of the *Taller de Gráfica Popular* sculpture department in Mexico. She became a Mexican citizen, renouncing her American nationality. She regained it in 2006.

She combined African, Mexican, and women's themes, especially Black American. She also explored social injustices and mother/child relationships.

Materials that she worked with included: cedar, eucalyptus, limestone, mahogany, marble and onyx.

She said, "I learned how you use your art for the service of people, struggling people, to whom only realism is meaningful."

44. Rachel Ruysch
Born 3 June 1664 The Hague, Netherlands
Died 12 October 1750 Amsterdam, Netherlands

Painter

As a child she practiced her drawing skills using her father's animal skeletons and flowers and minerals from his collection. Although he was also a painter, she exceeded his ability and became his teacher.

She was a student of Willem van Aelst, a Dutch artist known for his still lifes of flowers and game, until he died in 1683. However, she developed her own techniques that led to her working with horticulturists. Her work was sold internationally.

When she married another artist, they had ten children.

During seven decades, she is credited with painting 250+ canvases.

Although she was considered a "lesser" painter because of her subject, she became court painter to the Elector Palatine in Düsseldorf. "Greater" painters worked with historical and religious themes.

45. Augusta Christine Fells Savage
Born 29 February 1892 Green Cove Springs, Florida
Died 27 March 1962 New York, New York of cancer

Activist for Equal Rights
Laundry Worker
Sculptor

"My father kicked me four or five times a week ... and almost whipped all the art out of me. He thought art was a sin," Savage said.

Fortunately, when she changed to a West Palm Beach school, the principal encouraged her.

She married at 15, the first of three husbands. To earn money, she worked in a laundry.

When in 1919 at the Palm Beach County Fair she won a $25 prize for her work. She used this to search for commissions prior to going to New York.

Her scholarship to Fontainebleau School of Fine Arts in France was withdrawn when they learned she was black. However, she won a Cooper Union scholarship over 142 men.

The New York Public Library gave Savage her first commission, a bust of W.E.B. Du Bois. It led to more commissions.

Friends gave her money to study in Paris.

She was the first African American artist elected to the National Association of Women Painters and Sculptors.

46. Miriam Schapiro

Born 15 November Toronto, Canada
Died 20 June 2015 Hampton Bays, New York

Artist
Collagist
Feminist
Painter
Printmaker
Sculptor

Schapiro's grandfather invented a doll's moveable eye. She often incorporated dolls into her work which combined art with high-quality crafts. Dolls were just one of the feminist symbols she used in her work. Others included fans, flowers, hearts and the color pink.

Unlike many women artists, she received support from an early age, starting with her mother.

Later mentors included Victor d'Amico, Stuart Edie, James Lechaym and Mauricio Lasansk, as well as her artist father.

She married artist Paul Brach and moved with him when he was offered the position of painting instructor at Missouri University. She was given no post.

The couple moved to New York in 1951 where she found a better environment for her art.

She worked to have forgotten women artists recognized.

She collaborated with Judy Chicago on the Feminist Art Project.

47. Amrita Sher-Gil
Born 30 January 1913 Budapest, Hungary
Died 5 December 1941 Lahore, India thought to be from a failed abortion

Artist
Musician

Sher-Gil began art lessons at eight but had been painting since she was five. She was the child of an Indian aristocratic-scholar and a Hungarian opera singer mother. Like many painters, she received the most recognition after her death at 28. As a child she painted household servants.

She was also a gifted piano player and violinist.

Although raised in Budapest, the family moved to India in 1921 for financial reasons.

Her work captured contemporary Indian culture. Her paintings now are some of the most expensive of any Indian woman painter.

Throughout her life, she travelled to many countries. She studied painting in Paris and was considered to have a maturity unusual for her age. She moved to Florence to be with a sculptor where she continued her studies at the art school Santa Annunziata.

A bit of a rebel, she was expelled from a convent school for saying she was an atheist.

48. Elisabetta Sirani
Born 8 January 1638 Bologna, Italy, Holy Roman Empire
Died 28 August 1665, Bologna, Italy, Holy Roman Empire

Artist

It could be considered a 17th century mystery. Elisabetta Sirani, an

Italian Baroque painter and printmaker, died at 27. At first it was thought she was poisoned by a maid, but it also could have been caused by a peptic ulcer. The cause was never proven.

Her training began under her father's less than enthusiastic tutoring, some of which was her own observations rather than his direct teaching. A family friend claimed he helped call awareness to her talent.

Her reputation quickly exceeded that of her parent.

She became one of the first renowned women artists and founded a women's artists academy.

Despite her short life, she produced over 200 paintings and hundreds of drawings. Much of her work was signed, which was not a common practice at the time.

49. Sophie Henriette Gertrud Taeuber-Arp
Born 19 January 1889 Davos, Switzerland
Died 13 January 1943 Zurich, Switzerland of carbon monoxide poisoning

Architect
Artist
Dancer
Furniture and Interior designer
Puppeteer
Sculpture
Textile designer

Taeuber-Arp, a multi-talented artist, worked in many mediums. She is best known for her concrete art, geometric abstractions and her connection with the Dada movement.

Her mother taught her to sew. She studied textile design for four years at *Gewerbeschule* in St. Gallen (1906–1910) and at the

Kunstgewerbeschule in Hamburg (1914).

She danced with the Laban School in Zurich.

Taeuber-Arp taught embroidery and design at *Zürich Kunstgewerbeschule* (1912-1929).

Her textile work reflected the Dada movement, a movement rejecting modern capitalistic society by expressing nonsense and irrationality.

She performed as a dancer, choreographer and puppeteer.

Her husband was Dada artist Jean Arp. They shared many projects until her accidental death in 1943 from carbon monoxide poisoning when she stayed at a summer house.

ASTRONOMERS

The International Astronomical Union has a project: Women and Girls in Astronomy designed to "encourage everyone on and off the gender spectrum to consider careers in astronomy." They focused activities and awareness around the 2024 United Nations International Day of Women and Girls in Science.

50. Williamina Fleming
Born 15 May 1877 Dundee, Scotland
Died 15 December 1922 Boston, Massachusetts of pneumonia

Astronomer

She went from being a maid working for an astronomer to being one. Edward Pickering, an astronomer with a major project, hired Fleming, his maid, to supervise other women to help classify stars using a system of colors created by light reflected through a prism.

She headed up the privately funded Draper Catalogue project. The result organized over 10,000 stars.

Things did not go smoothly. Her approach was simplicity and created some dissension among others on the project. Her system used hydrogen and became known as the Pickering-Fleming system.

Harvard made her the Curator of Astronomical Photographs.

Fleming was always a proponent of women working in the field. (See below: Henrietta Leavitt, who worked on the same projects.)

Fleming is credited with the discovery of 310 stars, 10 novae and 59 gaseous nebulae.

51. Caroline Lucretia Herschel
Born 16 March 1750 Hanover, Germany
Died 9 January 1848 Hanover, Germany

Astronomer

For centuries women in the sciences could not earn a salary. Herschel was the first woman to receive pay as a scientist and the first woman in England to hold a government position. She discovered several comets, including 35P/Herschel–Rigollet.

Illness hampered her growth. She was four foot three. Her vision in her left eye was reduced. Although her late father wanted her to be educated, it was only through her brother's support that she went to England and took singing lessons in the hopes of becoming a singer. The duo also opened a millinery shop that failed.

As the younger sister of astronomer William Herschel, Royal Astronomer to George III, she worked with him throughout her career. She helped him in the making of telescopes while developing a record-keeping system. Her relationship with her brother became strained when he married and his wife resented Caroline, who had to adapt to her new status.

She was also the first woman to publish scientific findings in the Philosophical Transactions of the Royal Society, to be awarded a Gold Medal of the Royal Astronomical Society.

52. Margaretha (Maria) Kirch
Born 25 February 1670 Panitzsch, Germany
Died 29 December 1720 Berlin, Prussia of a fever

Astronomer

Kirch was the first woman to discover a comet, a discovery for which her husband claimed credit. He admitted it was his wife in 1710.

Her father, a Lutheran minister, believed his daughter should be well educated. After he died, her uncle saw to her education being continued.

Eventually, she worked with astronomer Christoph Armold, through whom she met her husband astronomer Gottfried Kirch. They married in 1692 and together they published calendars that gave astronomical information.

When Gottfried died, Kirch wanted to continue production, but the Royal Berlin Academy of Sciences felt it would be embarrassing to have a woman doing that work despite the fact she'd been doing it all along. Another astronomer with less experience was given the position.

Kirch was allowed to stay in the housing provided for them until 1717 when the Academy felt she was too prominent in observatory life, especially at public functions.

She refused to work for Russian Czar, Peter the Great.

Kirch wrote a number of papers accurately predicting future astronomical events.

53. Henrietta Leavitt
Born 4 July 1888 Lancaster, Massachusetts
Died 12 December 1921 Cambridge, Massachusetts of stomach
cancer

Astronomer

Edward Pickering knew he needed exceptional women to help count/compute stars. Funding came from private donors. He needed people who would work for little pay. He hired women including Leavitt. The women were great, cheap employees. (See Williamina Fleming, who headed the project).

She was first exposed to astronomy in her fourth year of university. Working with other women there was criticism of how proper it was. A *Boston Globe* article wrote, "These young women deal with difficult problems quite as successfully as do the men in other observatories." The article included a note of skepticism: "To be sure, not all women are capable of working in this field for the work demands special mental qualities . . ."

54. Nicole-Reine Lepaute
Born 5 January 1723 Luxembourg Palace, Paris, France
Died 6 December 1788 Paris, France

Astronomer
Clockmaker
Mathematician
Writer

Lepaute was lucky. She met men who supported, used and valued her abilities.

As a child, she was considered precocious, a fanatical reader and was fascinated with the stars.

In 1748, she married Jean-Pierre Lepaute, a royal clockmaker. She combined wifely duties such as keeping household accounts while describing her husband's inventions. Together they wrote *Traité d'Horlogerie.* Unlike many men, although her name wasn't listed as an author, her husband gave her credit for her contributions.

Working with Alexis Clairaut and Joseph Lalande, they predicted the return of Halley's Comet by calculating the timing. They also created solar eclipse and star catalogs.

Lepaute combined traditional views of women's roles while recognizing they might have intellectual abilities.

She became a member of the Scientific Academy of Béziers.

Lepaute has had both an asteroid and a lunar crater named after her.

55. Vera Florence Cooper Rubin
Born 23 July 1928 Philadelphia, Pennsylvania
Died 25 December 2016 Princeton, New Jersey of dementia complications

Astronomer

Rubin was pregnant when she wanted to present a paper on early evidence of the plane at the American Astronomical Society. She was refused.

When Rubin was an undergraduate at Vassar, she was the only woman studying astronomy. She would go on to discover discrepancies and deviations between the angular motion of galaxies by studying galactic rotation curves. Her pioneering research on dark matter and galaxy rotation rates was later substantiated.

It was often hard. Princeton turned her down for her gender, but she was able to earn graduate degrees from Cornell and Georgetown Universities. When she worked at the Carnegie Institute, Rubin needed to create her own women's facilities.

She did receive some recognition during her lifetime. The *New York Times* said she "ushered in a Copernican-scale change" in cosmological theory. The National Academy of Science accepted her as the second woman astronomer to receive the honor.

As a woman scientist, she did all she could to promote other women.

56. Beatrice Muriel Hill Tinsley
Born 27 January 1941 Chester, England
Died 23 March 1981 New Haven, Connecticut of melanoma

Astronomer
Cosmologist

Tinsley found university rules stifling. When married to a faculty physicist, she was prevented from working at his university. When her husband worked at the future University of Texas/ Dallas, she refused to follow the custom of hosting faculty teas.

Continuing her own studies at the University of Texas, she found herself the only woman. Her research was groundbreaking, but Tinsley was unable to find a permanent academic position until Yale hired her as its first astronomy professor. She left her husband and two adopted children to take the post.

Her research increased understanding of the life cycle of galaxies.

The American Astronomical Society awarded her the Annie J. Cannon Award in Astronomy, for "outstanding research and promise for future research by a postdoctoral woman researcher." They later established a prize in her honor.

Many honors followed her death, including a New Zealand postage stamp.

ATHLETES

Women in sports are a relatively new phenomenon. Granted, Mary Queen of Scots loved golf. Tennis might be enjoyed or a game of croquet, but mountain climbing, racing, team sports, bike riding were not for those gentle creatures which were far too delicate to participate in. Some even said sports could hurt women's fertility. Even if they wanted to play, their modest clothing made it difficult. How things have changed.

57. Annie Cohen Kopchovsky
Born 1870 Latvia
Died 11 November 1947 of a stroke

Bicycle Rider
Speaker
Writer

When told a woman couldn't bike around the world, Kopchovsky proved them wrong. Some of her travels had been by ship and train though. It had to do with an alleged wager (later proved a fake) when Paul Jones (pseudonym) allegedly made a $5,000 bet no woman could do it.

Pope Manufacturing, which made bicycles, jumped on board and selected Kopchovsky, an unlikely candidate. She was married, mother of three and Jewish. She agreed to use the less Jewish-sounding name Londonberry.

Her bike riding experience was minimal. She was tiny.

She started from the Massachusetts State House on 27 June 1894. She finished in October 1895 and covered North America, Asia and Europe. She raised money by selling advertising space on her bike.

There were hardships with her bike being confiscated and she was insulted for her appearance in France. She was ill in Sweden.

She lectured on her experiences and wrote *The New Woman*.

58. Marie Marvingt

Born 20 February 1875 Aurillac, France.
Died 14 December 1963 Meurthe-et-Moselle, France

Athlete
Aviator
Balloonist
Journalist
Nurse

Marvingt seems to have done it all: climbed the Swiss and French Alps, broke balloon records, been a certified flight and surgical nurse, helped establish an air ambulance service, and participated in bobsledding, canoeing, cycling, fencing, golf, gymnastics, riding, shooting, skating, skiing, and swimming.

Her father, a postmaster, loved sports. Her mother died when she was 14 leaving her to run the household.

Her nickname was "The Red Amphibian" after she swam the Seine through Paris. No wonder the French Academy of Sports gave her the only multi-sport medal they ever awarded.

She was the first woman to hold four pilot's licenses at the same time.

Later she broke her own record when she flew the longest distance for a woman in a nonstop flight.

Until she was discovered, she served as a male soldier in World

War I. She was the first woman to fly combat missions.
In World War II she served as a nurse.

ATOMIC BOMB VICTIM

The estimates are that between 90,000 and 120,00 people died in the Hiroshima bombing with many of the survivors developing radiation-caused illnesses well afterward.

59. Sadako Sasaki
Born 7 January 1943 Kusunoki Yamaguchi, Japan
Died 25 October 1955 Hiroshima, Japan of leukemia

Girl of 1,000 paper cranes

The girl, who survived the atomic Hiroshima bombing, made one thousand origami cranes as she was dying from the delayed result of the Hiroshima bombing although her leukemia symptoms had not appeared for ten years.

Her mother called it the "atomic bomb disease."

Sasaki heard the legend that whoever completes 10,000 cranes will have their wish granted. It was difficult for her to find enough paper and often sought hospital paper or gift wrap from other patients.

Her last words were "It's tasty" after eating tea on rice.

Her body was used by the Atomic Bomb Casualty Commission for research of the long-term effects of an atomic bomb on humans.

AVIATION

Women have always had a very small part to play in aviation whether behind the controls or turning the screwdriver. Today, about five percent of commercial pilots are women. For many, the urge to fly was almost as strong as the urge to breathe. There were other roles that they performed as well.

60. Florence Lowe "Pancho" Barnes

Born 22 July 1901 Pasadena, California
Died 30 March 1975 Boron, California of breast cancer

Aviator
Restaurant/bar owner
Stunt Pilot
Union Founder

The nickname Pancho came from her time in Mexico with revolutionaries. During that period, she dressed as a man.

Back in California, when driving her cousin to a flying lesson, she decided she wanted to fly. An excellent student, she soloed after only six hours of instruction.

Union Oil sponsored her. While working for them in 1930, she broke Amelia Earhart's air speed record.

Her next career step was to become a stunt pilot in Hollywood where she founded the Associated Motion Picture Pilots, which helped standardize safety and pay.

During the Depression she lost most of her wealth. She moved to the Mojave Dessert and opened the Happy Bottom Rising Club, a bar and restaurant frequented by several well-known pilots.

She had a major conflict with the United States Air Force which wanted her land for a runway without paying a fair price. It helped her court case that the USAF called her a prostitute and she won enough money to start over.

61. Sophie Blanchard
Born 25 March 1778 Trois Canons now Yves, France
Died 6 July 1819 Paris, France in a balloon crash

Balloonist

Sophie Blanchard, the first woman to pilot her own balloon, helped Napoleon plan a balloon attack and then convinced him it wouldn't work because of winds.

She married Jean-Pierre Blanchard, the world's first professional balloonist. Despite her fears of loud noises, carriage rides and more, she was never afraid when in a balloon calling it an "incomparable sensation."

When the couple were in need financially, they thought a female balloonist might attract paying customers.

Her husband died in 1808 from a heart attack after falling from a balloon.

Despite the accidents, she continued flying.

She skimped on the type of balloon to save money. Her smallness allowed her to use less propane gas.

Louis XVIII called her the "Official Aeronaut of the Restoration."

Her death was caused when her balloon caught fire.

62. Georgia Ann "Tiny" Thompson Broadwick
Born 8 April 1893 Oxford, North Carolina
Died 1978 buried in Henderson, North Carolina

Balloonist
Factory Worker
Inventor
Parachutist

Nicknamed Tiny because she was under five feet, she was the first woman to jump from airplanes.

She was married at 12, had a child at 13 and was deserted by her husband at 14.

She worked in a cotton mill to support herself and her child.

When she attended a Charles Broadwick aeronautic show, she saw people jumping from balloons and knew that was what she wanted to do. Broadwick adopted her and she made her first jump in 1908.

Not all her jumps worked. She broke bones and even jumped to save herself from a balloon fire.

In 1914 she taught the U.S. Army about parachutes.

After a line was caught on the airplane she was jumping from, she invented the rip cord to give herself control.

Forced to retire at 29 because of her ankles, she is said to have made over 1,100 jumps, including being the first woman to jump into water.

63. Bessie Coleman
Born 26 January 1892 Atlanta, Texas
Died 30 April 1926 Jacksonville, Florida airplane accident

Aviator

Coleman grew up picking cotton but wanted to fly. American flight schools admitted neither women nor African Americans.

By saving her money and a scholarship, she attended a French flight school and learned to fly a Nieuport 564 biplane. Determined to polish her skills, Coleman spent two months taking lessons from a French ace pilot near Paris.

In September 1921, she sailed for America.

To earn money, she became a stunt flyer in air shows and was given the nickname Queen Bess.

She refused to appear in any show forbidding African Americans from attending.

The *Fédération Aéronautique Internationale* issued her an international aviation license, the first black woman and the first Native American to receive one.

To finance buying her own plane, she opened a beauty parlor. The plane she bought was a Curtiss JN-4: however, it became her death vehicle because a wrench had jammed the controls. The plane went into a dive and Coleman was thrown from the plane at 3000 feet, dying instantly.

64. Sabiha Gökçen
Born 22 March 1913 Bursa, Ottoman Empire
Died 22 March 2001 Ankara, Turkey of heart failure

Aviator
Writer

Gökçen is considered to be the first female fighter pilot and flew in 32 military operations with over 8,000 hours of flying time.

When Turkey's first president Mustafa Kemal Atatürk visited Bursa, 12-year-old Gökçen asked to see him. He adopted her. When he took her to an airshow, she decided to be a pilot.

After her sister's death she was severely depressed and stopped activities until Atatürk insisted that she return. He had plans for her to be the first woman military pilot.

She flew a plane for the first time in 1936.

She went to a special training program because women were not accepted at Turkish war academies.

About her military flights she said, "They gave us the order, 'Shoot every living thing you see'; we were firebombing even the goats which were the food of the rebels."

She became a chief trainer at Türkkuşu Flight School.

She wrote the book *A Life Along the Path of Atatürk*.

65. Joy Lofthouse
Born 14 February 1923 Cirencester, England
Died 15 November 2017 England

Pilot

They were called Spitfire Girls and Attagirls and Lofthouse was one of them. She learned to fly a plane before she learned to drive.

There were 168 female pilots among the 1,153 male pilots who flew Barracuda bombers, Mustang Fighters and Spitfires during World War II.

Of the original group, 156 lost their lives.

Her first flying lesson in 1943 was part of the Air Transport Auxiliary (ATA) in a Spitfire.

Her main job was to fly the aircraft from factory to airfield. She was said to have flown 18 different types of airplanes.

She became a teacher after the war. Her second husband was a Royal Air Force pilot.

To commemorate VE Day in 2015 at age 70 she had a chance to get into the cockpit of the single-engine Spitfire. She declared "[It is] the nearest thing to having wings of your own and flying."

66. Betty Ann Ong
Born 5 February 1956 San Francisco, California
Died 11 September 2001 in a plane crash

Flight Attendant

In an eight-minute 26-second conversation between Flight 11 and American Airlines, Ong notified the hijacking that was part of 9/11.
The FAA closed airspace.

It wasn't her first crisis. During a robbery at the family factory, she remained calm when a gun was held to her head. Another time she had responded to a car being hit by a truck and ran to help the passengers.

During the conversation she was able to report to the ground the seat numbers of the hijackers.

During the hijacking it was impossible to open the cockpit door.

67. Marina Popovich
Born 30 July 1931
Died 30 November 2017 Boulder, Colorado

Air Force Colonel
Engineer
Test Pilot
Writer

As the first Soviet woman (and third woman worldwide) to break the sound barrier, she set 100+ aviation records flying 40 different types of aircraft. Her nickname was "Madame MiG."

She learned to fly as a child but was barred from being a military pilot after World War II. Not happy with barriers, at 16 and claiming she was 22, she asked for a reversal of the rule. Her wish was granted. She graduated from Novosibirsk Aviation Technicum in 1951.

Starting as an engineer, she then became a test pilot.

Her first husband was Pavel Popovich, a cosmonaut aboard the Vostok 4 in 1962.

She joined the Soviet Air Forces and in 1964 became a military test pilot. In 1978 she entered the military reserves. She worked as a test pilot for the Ukrainian Antonov Design Bureau, which specialized in large airplanes using unprepared runways.

She wrote nine books, two screenplays and a poetry collection.

A Cancer constellation star was named for her.

68. Irina Fyodorovna Sebrova

Born 25 December 1914 Novomoskovsk, Tula Governorate, Russia
Died 5 April 2000 Moscow, Russia

Aviator
Bomber Pilot
Locksmith

Sebrova flew 1,008 missions as part of the 46th Taman Guards Night Bomber Aviation Regiment during World War II. Some nights she flew several missions.

Her family was poor and had six children. They moved to Moscow where she attended a trade school. Her original career was as a locksmith, but she had other factory jobs.

In 1939 she graduated from the Kherson School of Flight Instructors and then became an instructor before training at the Engels Military Aviation School of Pilots.

She was said to remain calm during major problems such as when an engine failed. She landed the stricken plane behind enemy lines then walked through a forest until she found Soviet troops.

She flew more missions than any other woman pilot over Belorussia, Caucasus, Crimea, Germany, Kuban, Poland, Ukraine.

Her highest rank was lieutenant, and she remained in the military until 1948.

BAD WOMEN

Why bad women? If becoming a professional woman throughout history has been difficult, "succeeding" in crime was also difficult. The causes for a life of crime are not dissimilar to what drives a woman to select a different path than conventional womanhood. Also, there are women who are considered "bad" such as witches and prostitutes who are victims of the society in which they live.

69. Anne Bonny
Born March 1697 exact date unknown near Cork, Ireland
Disappeared April 1721

Pirate

In history there are few female pirates.

Anne is thought to be the illegitimate daughter of a lawyer and maid, but her father took custody. She moved first to London then to Carolina.

As a redhead living up to the stereotype of redheads having a temper, she is said to have stabbed a servant when she was a teen. One story claims she set fire to her father's plantation.

Her husband James Bonny was a minor pirate. Bonny took Calico Jack Rackham as a lover and co-pirate. They operated mainly in the Caribbean. Along with Mary Read, the three were captured in October 1720, tried in Jamaica and sentenced to death.

Several women ". . . pleaded their bellies." One died of a fever, another was hung, but the exact end of Bonny is unknown although she may have been released and returned to South Carolina.

70. Leonarda Cianciulli
Born 18 April 1894 Montella, Italy
Died 15 October 1970 Naples, Italy of cerebral apoplexy

Serial killer

Cianciulli was called the Soap Maker of Correggio because she turned her three murder victims into soap.

A fortune teller's reading predicted unhappy events and misfortune. As a child she tried to kill herself twice.

She believed her mother had cursed her marriage to a registry office clerk.

Of the 17 children she bore, only four survived.

Her home in Lacedonia, Avellino was destroyed in a 1930 earthquake.

When her eldest son was about to enter the Royal Italian Army, she was convinced only human sacrifice would protect him. She selected three local middle-aged women: Faustina Setti, Francesca Soavi and Virginia Cacioppo.

After she convinced the women to write postcards talking about their future travels, she drugged them, and then made parts of them into soap. With other parts she added the ingredients for cake.

Some sources record that Cianciulli apparently received money from her victims.

She was sentenced to 30 years in prison, where she died.

71. Nexhmije Hoxha
Born 8 February 1921 Bitola, Kingdom of Serbs, Croats and Slovenes

Died 26 February 2020 Tirana, Albania

An Albanian Communist Politician
First Secretary of the Party of Labour of Albania.

So many questions about who and what she was.
- Was Nexhmije Hoxha a Lady MacBeth
  responsible for ordering the deaths of her
  countrymen?
- Was the name Balkan Red Widow better suited?
- Was she a patriotic leader fighting Fascism in
  World War II?
- Did her pro-feminist stance do more than eliminate
  the veil for women?
- Did she embezzle 750,000 leks for which she served
  four years of an amended 11-year sentence? Did she
  live extravagantly as her fellow Albanians starved?

What is known was that she was important in her own right
as Director of the Institute of Marxist–Leninist Studies, the
organization responsible for purity and propaganda. Her training had
been in education.

The wife of the former Albanian leader, pro-Stalinist Enver Hoxha,
was probably some or all of them. It is unusual for the spouse of a
leader to wield power and she did.

72. Catherine Monvoisin known as "La Voisin"
Born c. 1640
Executed 22 February 1680 by burning

Abortionist
Fortune Teller
Poisoner

La Voisin headed a network of Parisian fortune tellers which also took commissions in black magic, poison distribution and abortion providing. The network may have been responsible for 1000 to 25,000 deaths.

Claims that unborn fetuses were burned was never proven.

Her husband Antoine Monvoisin, a Parisian silk merchant and jeweler, went bankrupt leaving her to provide for the family of seven by fortune telling. Marriage did not stop her from having prominent lovers.

She developed a lucrative practice with aristocratic clients. Among her clients was Madame de Montespan, the official royal mistress to King Louis XIV of France.

Using bones of toads, moles, teeth, iron filings and other ingredients her business included the sale of her homemade love potions.

For clients who wanted poison, she provided that as well.

She was arrested and tried, but never tortured out of fear which clients she might name.

73. Grace O'Malley "Grainne Ni Mhaille"
Born c 1530 Umhaille, Ireland
Died c 1603 Rockfleet Castle, Ireland

Pirate
Legends

When Grace was told by her father that she couldn't go to sea because of her long hair, she cut it.

The Uí Mháilles were a powerful seafaring clan with castles facing the sea as protection. They were known for piracy.

Upon her father's death, Grace took over.

Income, also called Black Rents, was obtained from people living on the family lands.

When the English encroached on her power, she petitioned Queen Elizabeth I whom she is said to have met. The queen granted Grace certain provisions in return for some lands of the O'Malley family.

She was said to be multi-lingual, speaking in various degrees French, English, Spanish, Scots and Gaelic.

74. Gertrud Emma Scholtz-Klink (Maria Stuckbrock)
Born 9 February 1902 Adelsheim, Germany
Died 24 March 1999 Tübingen Bebenhausen, Germany

Nazi party member

In complete contrast to those fighting for women's right, Scholtz-Klink's role as Reich's Women's *Führerin* was to enshrine women's role as a good *Hausfrau*. As a Nazi party member, she was appointed leader of the Nazi's Women's league by Adolf Hitler.

She, herself, was the mother of six children before her first husband, a factory worker, left her a widow. Later she was married to Dr. Günther Scholtz for six years before they divorced.

She fought against women in politics, although she was in politics. Male politicians paid her little heed. Schlotz-Klink was quoted as saying "the mission of woman is to minister in the home and in her profession to the needs of life from the first to last moment of man's existence."

Women's organizations established programs to teach family and household management.

Her third husband was *SS-Obergruppenführer* August Heissmeyer. At war's end, they hid near Tübingen and were arrested three years later. She was sentenced to four years in prison.

75. Valerie Jean Solanas
Born 9 April 1936 Ventor City, New Jersey
Died 25 April 1988 San Francisco of pneumonia

Attempted Murderer
Feminist
Writer

Solanas, in June 1968, shot artist Andy Warhol and art critic Mario Amaya. Both survived. She attempted but failed to shoot Fred Hughes, Warhol's manager.

She was angry at Warhol because he had claimed to have lost her script for *Up Your Ass,* a play she wanted him to produce. She also blamed Warhol for colluding with a Parisian publisher specializing in censored works, who had offered a contract. She thought they might be trying to steal her work.

She turned herself into the police and received a three-year prison sentence which included treatment for paranoid schizophrenia in a mental hospital.

Her publications were *SCUM Manifesto, Society for Cutting Up Men,* promoting the ideas of eliminating the male sex and the money system.

How much of her attitude was shaped by an unhappy childhood and sexual abuse is not known.

Her degree was in psychology from Maryland University, College Park.

Her ideas have been labelled "unabashed misandry" or "prejudice against men."

76. Agnes Waterhouse
Born c. 1503
Executed for witchcraft 29 July 1566

One of many women accused of witchcraft in England, Mother Waterhouse, as she was called, was one of the first witches executed under the Witchcraft Act of 1562.

She had confessed to turning her white spotted cat named Satan into a toad. The cat had previously belonged to another witch, Elizabeth Francis. The cat was allegedly in exchange for a cake.

Although Waterhouse claimed to pray often, she said it was only in Latin. The cat had forbidden her to pray in English.

Her crimes included making William Fynne ill, killing livestock and her husband.

Her daughter Joan, accused of the same crime, was exonerated, although her testimony helped convict her mother. Information about the trial was recorded in a pamphlet "The examination and confession of certaine Wytches at Chensforde in the Countie of Essex before the Quenes Maiesties Judges the XXVI daye of July anno 1566."

77. Aileen Carol Wuornos
Born 29 February 1956 Rochester, Michigan
Executed 9 October 2002 Raiford, Florida by lethal injection

Prostitute
Serial killer

Wuornos robbed and murdered seven middle-aged clients between

1989–1990. She claimed self-defense.

One could say that she never stood a chance. Her parents were teenagers when she was born. Her father deserted her. Her mother bailed when Wuornos was four. Living with alcoholic grandparents did not improve her situation. She claimed her grandfather sexually assaulted her.

- At 11 she began trading sex for favors
- At 14 she had a son
- At 18 she was arrested for drunk driving
- At 22 she tried suicide

When her grandfather threw her out, she lived in the woods, supporting herself through prostitution.

In 1976 while living in Florida, she married a yacht club president, who was 69. The marriage was later annulled.

She received $10,000 in life insurance from her brother's death, which she used to pay fines.

Her life involved a series of petty and not so petty crimes.

Found guilty, she was executed.

BUSINESSWOMEN

Throughout history, men have ruled the business world, although some women have managed to start their own small enterprises and built them up. Only in the last few decades have women taken part in board rooms and in the top echelons: 15% were CEOs of Fortune 500 companies according to a report in March 2022 from the World Economic Forum. Women of color hold only 1%. The figures vary on how women have succeeded in the Business world. According to *Forbes Magazine,* 45% of the enrollees in MBA programs are women.

78. Helen Bates "Penny" Chenery
Born 27 January 1922 New Rochelle, New York
Died 16 September 2017 Boulder. Colorado of stroke complications

Businesswoman
Doughnut Girl (providing baked goods to soldiers)
Horse Woman

Her millionaire father may have helped Chenery open doors, but once inside she worked hard to accomplish her goals. He transmitted his love of horses and business acumen to her.

Earlier in her life, she was a Doughnut Girl during World War II.

Her father had founded Meadow Stables, which was in difficulty when Chenery, in 1968, took over as head.

The dream of winning the Kentucky Derby became a reality twice: Riva Ridge and Secretariat. She syndicated their breeding rights for over $11 million. Tax debts still forced her to sell Meadow Stables.

She moved the horses to New York.

She was the first woman to be admitted to the Jockey Club.

Her love of horses showed in her roles as president of the Thoroughbred Owners and Breeders Association and an American Horse Council Executive Committee Member. To save horses from mistreatment and death, she founded the Thoroughbred Retirement Foundation.

79. Madam C.J. Walker (Sarah Breedlove)
Born 23 December 1867 Delta, Louisiana
Died 25 May 1919 Irvington, New York from kidney failure

Activist
Businesswoman
Philanthropist

Under the name Madam C.J. Walker Manufacturing Company, Sarah Breedlove became the first self-made, African American millionaire. She developed and sold products for women of color.

She was the first child in her family born into freedom. Orphaned at seven, she became a domestic worker. It was at Sunday school that she learned to read.

Her own skin and hair problems led her to develop her products, which were sold door-to-door, then by direct mail.

Working with her husband, whom she later divorced, they used various selling techniques and also opened a beauty parlor to train salespeople to whom she granted licenses. Their sales gave these women economic independence. Some 20,000 women were said to work for her.

She became active politically in racial issues.

She donated to universities, churches and negro organizations.

CHEFS

Women dining in restaurants alone was called "sad" by *The Baltimore Sun*. Women chefs, if they existed at all were usually hidden away. There was a small shift in the late 19th century with the western states moving faster in that direction than the eastern. Cafeterias and tea rooms were more apt to have women chefs. According to writer Jan Whitaker, after World War II being an astronaut was a more promising career than being a chef.

80. Marella Hazan
Born 15 April 1924 Cesenatico, Emilia-Romagna, Italy
Died 29 September 2013 Longboat Key, Florida

Chef

When Hazan married in 1955, she had never cooked. It was part of her wifely responsibility, so she checked cookbooks for ideas, combining them with childhood memories.

Having worked as a science teacher, it was a natural step to give cooking lessons in her apartment.

After contributing recipes to the *New York Times*, she published *The Classic Italian Cookbook*. That and following cookbooks concentrated on classic Italian cooking, ignoring Anglo influences. She did substitute ingredients for those seldom found outside Italy.

Her methods preferred making items by hand such as pasta when possible.

Comments about her memories preceded some recipes. An example:

"On an afternoon slowed down by the southern sun, it was one of the best ways to while away the time, watching life dawdle by as you let the *granita*'s crystals melt on the tongue, spoonful by spoonful, until the roof of your mouth felt like an ice cavern pervaded by the aroma of strong coffee."

81. Marjorie Child Husted
Born 2 April 1892 Minneapolis, Minnesota
Died 23 December 1986 Minneapolis, Minnesota

Businesswoman
Brand Creator
Home Economist

"Management is dominated by men and there is no indication of interest on the part of employers for change." Although General Mills claimed Betty Crocker didn't exist, Husted was the driving force behind the name. Betty Crocker at one point was receiving 4,000 letters daily.

In 1929 she taught cooking around the country. She talked with cooks and housewives gathering information she would later use. Back in Minneapolis she headed up GM's 40-person Home Service Department which would answer customer questions.

She made Betty Crocker a household name by radio, television, books, and newspaper articles.

When people visited GM, they would meet Betty Crocker as played by Husted.

There was a three-step process before recipes were issued to the public. Home economists tested it, then local housewives and finally it was tested across the country.

Husted wrote all the five-minute radio shows, *Time for Betty Crocker*. Not bad for a person whom management said didn't exist.

82. Ruth Graves Wakefield
Born 17 June 1903 East Walpole, Massachusetts
Died 10 January 1977 Plymouth, Massachusetts

Business owner
Chef
Dietician
Food Lecturer
Writer

We've probably all baked or eaten chocolate chip cookies without ever thinking of the recipe creator, Ruth Graves Wakefield.

Wakefield graduated from Framingham State College where she studied to be a dietician.

After marrying Kenneth Wakefield, a meat packing executive, she and her husband opened a tourist lodge, called Toll House Inn. Its restaurant quickly became popular. Wakefield cooked the meals using her grandmother's and her recipes.

She later wrote *Ruth Wakefield's Tried and True Recipes*.

To expand the flavors of the restaurant's cookie offerings, Wakefield experimented with hunks of chocolate in the cookie dough. Nestle's chocolate chips were found to be the best solution.

The cookies were publicized by General Mills home economist Marjorie Husted, a.k.a. Betty Crocker, and *Boston-Herald-Traveler* food editor Marjorie Mills, increasing their popularity until it became an internationally known taste delight.

During World War II, the restaurant shipped cookies to fighting men overseas.

Massachusetts designated the chocolate chip cookie as its official state cookie.

CHILDREN'S ADVOCATE

It was Congressman Robert Cramer who promoted the creation of Children's Advocacy Centers, bringing together different organizations in the legal, medical and social services. By 2011, they served 269,000 children. Fighting for the lives of children however had been the work of many women on a smaller scale.

83. Bertha Marian Holt
Born 5 February 1904 Des Moines, Iowa
Died 31 July 2000 Creswell, Oregon

Orphan Children's Advocate

Grandma Holt, as she was called, was a deeply religious woman. Religion gave her the support she would use through life in her work for orphans.

She trained as a nurse.

She and her husband, Henry Holt, did farm work while saving their money. They moved to Oregon, and through hard work became owners of a lumber mill with 53 employees.

After watching a film on Amerasian orphans in Korea, they wanted to adopt eight children but ran into the two foreign children adoptions limit. When the law changed, they adopted four boys and four girls of various ages.

Holt International Children Services was founded in 1964. It worked with an existing orphanage plus built a second. Grandma worked with other countries to establish foreign adoption programs.

CONSERVATIONIST

Conservationism combines political, social and environmental movements to preserve the world. Many conservationists focus on one aspect of the many problems facing the planet today. It might be a woman chaining herself to a tree or another speaking up at a small-town government meeting. The Nature Conservancy salutes women who have sacrificed their time and energy to gather evidence for needed reforms. In the early days when women wanted jobs in conservation they were told, "You're a woman; you're not allowed to have this job."

84. Dian Fossey

Born 16 January 1932 San Francisco, California
Murdered c 26 December 1985 Volcanoes National Park, Rwanda

Conservationist
Primatologist

A pet goldfish planted the seed for Fossey's love of animals.

Her life was marked with difficulties. Her stepfather, a strict disciplinarian, would not allow Fossey to eat with the family. She defined him by not going to business school and enrolling at California University's pre-veterinary school, enrolling at California University's pre-veterinary school. She failed her second year.

She switched to occupational therapy at San Jose State College. She said that her occupational training experience helped her with her life-long study of gorillas.

Louis Leaky helped her find funding for her long-term projects. Local political upheaval slowed her work.

She called gorillas "dignified, highly social, gentle giants, with individual personalities, and strong family relationships."

She financed poaching patrols that destroyed over 987 poacher traps. It was rumored that she attacked poachers. The killing of her favorite gorilla sent her into a depression.

She was killed in her cabin.

It is impossible to cram her life into a small biography. A movie was made from her book, *Gorillas in the Mist,* nominated for five Oscars.

COMPUTING EXPERTS

According to Wikipedia, "The gender disparity and the lack of women in computing from the late 20th century onward has been examined, but no firm explanations have been established." Still women have made major contributions before computers were part of everyday life, and their work made the next development steps possible.

85. Anita Borg

Born 17 January 1949 Chicago, Illinois
Died 6 April 2003 Sonoma, California of a brain tumor

Computer Scientist

Despite loving math, Borg never planned to go into computer science. She taught herself programming anyway. In 1981 she earned her Ph.D. in computer science from New York University.

She was a woman who supported other women in her field passionately by founding the Institute for Women and Technology, later renamed the Anita Borg Institute for Women and Technology, the Grace Hopper Celebration of Women in Computing and Systers, the first email network for women in technology.

Systers started in the ladies' room during a conference when the women noted how few females were there. To be a member, a woman needed to have highly technical training.

Although almost all projects were technical, members helped convince Mattel to remove the phrase, "Math class is tough" from Barbie's voice chip.

86. Grace Brewster Hopper

Born 9 December 1906 New York City, New York
Died 1 January 1992 Arlington County, Virginia in her sleep

Computer Scientist
Mathematician

When she retired from the United States Navy as a Rear Admiral, she had served longer than anyone.

She had been a computer programing pioneer with the attitude of not accepting that things were always done a certain way. She found a way to do them better.

Her Ph.D.s were in mathematics and mathematical physics from Yale University and Vassar.

When she first tried to enlist in the Navy at 34, she was rejected for age and not meeting height and weight requirements. She served in the Naval Reserve. She retired in 1966 and rejoined in 1967, finally retiring in 1986.

Her computer work was revolutionary, if not developing major concepts creating the steps that others followed. She wrote the 500-page "A Manual of Operation for the Automatic Sequence Controlled Calculator," the first computer manual, along with other major papers.

When she wanted to use English for programming, she was discouraged until she created the way for computers to turn word into code. During her lifetime she was awarded 40 honorary degrees.

The use of the word "bug" is credited to her after a moth caused a programming problem.

87. Augusta Ada King

Born 10 December 1815 London, England
Died 27 November 1852 London, England of uterine cancer

Computer Ancestor
Mathematician
Writer

King was the first to recognize that the Charles Babbage computer, on which she worked, might have applications beyond calculations, which is why she could be called the computer's ancestor.

Her mother pushed her mathematical interests, hopefully to counter the effects of King's father Lord Byron.

Despite childhood illnesses, she was an excellent student that continued throughout her life. "Poetical science" is how she described her studies and contributions.

Her marriage to the Earl of Lovelace William King, put her in the social circle of well-known scientists and writers.

She developed a working relationship with Charles Babbage, who originated the idea of the computer.

She raised questions, still needing to be answered today, on how society and technology interrelate.

88. Arfa Abdul Karim Randhawa

Born 2 February 1995 Faisalbad, Pakistan
Died 14 January 2012 Lahore, Pakistan of heart failure and an epileptic seizure

Computer Prodigy

In her 16 years, this computer prodigy racked up the professional recognition of being the youngest Microsoft Certified Professional

(MCP). Among her other awards was the Fatimah Jinnah Gold Medal in the field of Science and Technology and the Award for Pride of Performance.

Despite her youth, she represented her country on the international stage at various conferences.

An epileptic seizure caused brain damage in 2011. Bill Gates offered to do everything possible for her treatment. A panel of international doctors worked with her case, but she died on 14 January 2012 of cardiac arrest despite showing some improvement.

CRIMINOLOGIST

Despite that most popular mystery novels and detective programs don't discuss criminology theory very much, solving a crime taps into many disciplines including anthropology, behavioral science, biology, economics, laws, pathology, psychiatry, psychology, social work and more, depending on the crime.

89. Frances Glessner Lee
Born 25 March 1878 Chicago, Illinois
Died 27 January 1962 Bethlehem, New Hampshire

Forensic Scientist

What would all the TV police shows or homicide detectives do if Lee hadn't existed?

Fascinated by Sherlock Holmes when she was child, her gender shut her out of studying forensic science.

To learn more about medicine in relation to murder, she shadowed private medical practitioners.

She created the 20 doll-house-sized crime scene dioramas called *Nutshell Studies of Unexplained Death*, which were used to train homicide detectives. They were based on real crimes and autopsies which she had attended. Eighteen are still in use as well as being considered works of art.

Thanks to inherited money, Lee helped to establish the Department of Legal Medicine at Harvard University and endowed the Magrath Library of Legal Medicine there.

She became the first female police captain in the United States.

DANCER

Every culture has some type of dancing, the movement of the body to music. The forms are as varied as the human imagination, often reflecting the culture that created them.

90. Ayu Bulantrisna Djelantaik
Born 8 September 1947 Deventer, Netherlands
Died 24 February 2021 Jakarta, Indonesia of pancreatic cancer

Dancer
Doctor

Being a leading Balinese dancer and doctor is a strange combination of careers, but Djelantik achieved both.

Her Indonesia father met her Dutch mother when he was in The Netherlands. He was a malaria specialist but insisted his children learn classical Balinese dances. She combined both cultures.

She performed classical legong dances with her dance troupe. Legong dances combine intricate footwork, finger movements and exaggerated facial expressions.

Dedicated to the arts, she also supported children's literature and film making.

She studied and lectured in her specialty otolaryngology. She served as chair of the Southeast Asia Society for Sound Hearing.

The dance studio she founded, Bengkel Tari Ayu Bulan, is still active today. YouTube has some of their videos.

ECONOMISTS

Economics is a social science that explains society in terms of production and distribution of services. The information it shares has the power to bring about good and bad changes depending on prevailing theories. According to the American Economic Association, 15% of full professors in economics departments and 31% of faculty at the assistant level are women. Some 22% of tenured and tenure-track faculty in economics are women.

91. Sadie Tanner Mossel Alexander
Born 2 January 1898 Philadelphia, Pennsylvania
Died 1 November 1987 Philadelphia, Pennsylvania of Alzheimer's complications

Civil Rights Activist
Economist

As an African American, Mossell Alexander specialized in breaking barriers. At the University of Pennsylvania, she faced many problems including false plagiarism accusations.

The denial of membership by Phi Beta Kappa was not rectified until 1970.

Her studies were in education, economics and law. She was the first African American to receive a Ph.D. in economics in the United States, and the first to receive a law degree from the University of Pennsylvania Law School.

Her husband, Raymond Pace Alexander, a son of former slaves, graduated from Harvard Law School. They formed their own law firm.

In 2022, Alexander was named a distinguished fellow by the American Economic Association, the first and only economist to receive the honor posthumously for her contributions to economic equality and civil rights.

She served on many high-level government commissions and committees working on human and civil rights issues from 1940 to 1979.

92. Emily Greene Balch

Born 8 January 1867 Jamaica Plain, Massachusetts
Died January 1961 Cambridge, Massachusetts

Economist
Editor
Sociologist
Pacifist
Professor

Balch used her education from Bryn Mawr, Harvard and University of Chicago in several areas. Parisian graduate work led to her publication: *Public Assistance of the Poor in France*.

Back in the States, she worked with settlements collaborating with Jane Addams.

At Wellesley College, she became an Associate Professor, then Professor of Political Economy and of Political and Social Science. After Wellesley terminated her contract, she edited *The Nation*.

Her lifelong interests included poverty, child labor and immigration.

As a pacifist, she was the Secretary-Treasurer of the Switzerland-based Women's International League for Peace and Freedom.

She was a leader of the Women's Trade Union League. She helped create peace summer schools with branches in 50+ countries. Working with the League of Nations, she worked on drug control, aviation, refugees, and disarmament issues.

In World War II, she favored Allied victory but supported conscientious objector rights.

93. Edith Abbott

Born 26 September 1876 Grand Island, Nebraska
Died 28 July 1957 Grand Island, Nebraska

Economist
Educator
Humanitarian
Social Worker
Statistician
Writer

Abbott combined her pioneering in social work, social reform with her background in economics. Her parents, a father that was a Lieutenant Governor and her mother as an abolitionist and suffragist, were great influences especially in the value of women's rights.

When she could not afford to attend university, took night courses and eventually won a fellowship at Chicago University where she received her Ph.D. in economics. She also studied at University College London and the London School of Economics. While in London, she lived in a social reformers' settlement. Later she would live in Jane Addams's Hull House.

She believed that statistics were the route to social reform. She published "Statistics Relating to Crime in Chicago," in collaboration with Sophonisba Breckinridge. Other publications included:
> • The Tenements of Chicago, 1908–1935
> • The Delinquent Child and the Home

• Attendance in the Chicago Schools
• Social Welfare and Professional Education

Throughout her career she worked on developing humane welfare policies for the poor no matter what their national origin.

She was Dean of the School of Social Service Administration, Chicago University.

EDUCATORS

The saying that those who can do do, and those who can't teach is so very false. Teaching can be not just a skill, but an art, spreading ideas and inspiring others to be the best they can be. Teaching was a profession that was more open to women at least at the early classroom level.

94. Nannie Helen Burroughs
Born 2 May 1879 Orange, Virginia
Died 20 May 1961 Washington, D.C.

Civil rights activist
Educator
Feminist
Orator
Playwriter
Religious Leader

Burroughs believed that African American women should learn more than domestic skills. She opened the National Training School in 1908, providing the first 31 women access to education and skills including business and agriculture. Since then, the school has educated hundreds of women.

The daughter of freed slaves, Burroughs moved with her parents to Washington, D.C. There, while attending high school, she organized the Harriet Beecher Stowe Literary Society.

Upon graduation, she couldn't find work as a domestic-science teacher because of her dark skin.

In Kentucky from 1898-1909, she was editorial secretary/ bookkeeper for the Foreign Mission Board, National Baptist Convention.

Over the years, she was affiliated with many organizations, all promoting women, including the National Association of Colored Women (NACW) 100+ women's clubs strong and the National Association of Wage Earners.

She worked in Herbert Hoover's Administration on housing issues.

She wrote plays which were performed for amateur church theatrical groups: *The Slabtown District Convention* and *Where is My Wandering Boy Tonight?*

95. Dorothea Frances Canfield
Born 17 February 1879 Lawrence, Kansas
Died 9 November 1958 Arlington, Vermont of a cerebral
hemorrhage

Artist
Educator
Writer

Canfield was one of the first educators to bring the Montessori methods to the U.S.

The first woman to receive an honorary degree from Dartmouth, she received six degrees from six universities.

She studied Romance languages at Paris University and Columbia where she received a doctorate.

With John Redwood Fisher, whom she married in 1907, she had two children – a daughter, Sally, and a son, Jimmy.

In 1911, Canfield Fisher visited the "children's houses" in Rome established by Maria Montessori. So impressed with the method, she joined the cause and translated Montessori's book into English. She wrote five of her own books: three nonfiction and two novels.

96. Septima Poinsette Clark
Born 3 May 1898 Charleston, South Carolina
Died 15 December 1987 Johns Island, South Carolina

Civil Rights Activist
Educator

"I never felt that getting angry would do you any good other than hurt your own digestion – keep you from eating, which I liked to do." Clark believed in action.

Education for a black child was difficult, but she managed to finish ninth grade at Avery Institute where she later taught.

On Johns Island, she taught illiterate adults at night using the Sears Catalog. She made $35 a week for her daytime teaching. The white teacher across the street made $85.

Defying her principal's orders, she collected signatures on a petition to let blacks become principals.

Her degrees were from Columbia University, Clark College and Hampton Institute. At one point she took morning and evening classes while teaching afternoons.

She joined the National Association for the Advancement of Colored People (NAACP). When she refused to give up her membership, she was fired.

As workshop director of the Highland Folk School in Tennessee, she created "citizenship schools." Some 700,000 people were registered to vote after attending these schools.

97. Sarah Fuller
Born 14 February 1836 Weston, Massachusetts
Died 1 August 1927 Newton Lower Falls, Massachusetts

Educator

Fuller was present when Alexander Graham Bell made that first famous telephone call. But her connection with him was in the training of teaching deaf children to speak. Her first teaching was with normal hearing children.

A three-month training course at the Clarke School for the Deaf in Northampton gave her the skills she needed to become principal of the Horace Mann School for the Deaf and Hard of Hearing, founded in 1869 by the Boston School Committee. It served 10 children when it opened but increased to 60 under Fuller's leadership.

She wrote *An Illustrated Primer* for deaf teachers and felt strongly that training of the deaf should begin as young as possible. She founded the American Association to Promote the Teaching of Speech to the Deaf in 1890.

In 1902 she founded the Home for Little Deaf Children and was principal until her retirement.

98. Nora Herlihy
Born 27 February 1910 Ballydesmond, Ireland
Died 7 February 1988 Daley, Ireland

Credit Union Founder
Educator
Reformer

The first meetings of the Irish Credit Union League were run in Herlihy's house. She may have failed as a missionary, which she wanted to be, but she succeeded as a teacher and as one of the founders of the Irish credit union movement which brought financial services to those who never had them before.

She saw credit unions as a solution to poverty and unemployment. Their goals combined socialism with market capitalism.

A tireless researcher, she looked to the National Credit Union Association in Wisconsin and travelled to the United States and Canada to learn more. She also knew it was necessary to educate the population in cooperative values without threatening any small business.

Throughout her credit union work she continued teaching at St. Joseph's Girls National School in Dublin.

Her lobbying helped pass the Credit Union Act of 1966.

As of 2018 Irish credit unions had €13.4 billion in savings and loans of almost €4.5 billion.

99. Mary Mason Lyon
Born 28 February 1797 Buckland, Massachusetts
Died 5 March 1849 South Hadley, Massachusetts of erysipelas

Educator

Mary Lyon believed in women's education and as founder of places such as the Ipswich, Wheaton and Mount Holyoke Female Seminaries, she had the chance to put her ideas into practice. She thought a women's curriculum should be as rigorous as men's.

Physical activity was also important to her. Students were required to walk a mile a day.

Wheaton and Mount Holyoke are now full colleges. She also believed that these institutions of learning should be affordable to girls of lower and middle classes as well as the elite.

Her father's death left her scrambling for her own education despite her farm chores.

When she was able to attend Byfield Seminary the headmaster and his assistance took her under their wing planting the seed for her lifelong dedication to women's education.

100. Charlotte Maria Shaw Mason
Born 1 January 1842 Bangor, Wales
Died 16 January 1923 Ambleside, Wales

Educator
Reformer

Her philosophy that every child should have access to a liberal curriculum was adapted in many schools. Her own education was at home where she was taught by her parents.

Her vision for education came from her teaching experiences. She translated that experience into teachers' guides and books. They were also for parents teaching their children at home.

She helped found the Parents' National Educational Union (PNEU) and served as the editor of the *Parents' Review*.

After moving to Ambleside, England she opened the House of Education to train those working with children.

She was a staunch supporter of scouting for children.

Her philosophy can be summarized by two of her quotes: "Education is an atmosphere, a discipline, a life" and "Education is the science of relations." Today Ambleside Online is a free homeschooling program using Mason's principles.

101. Margarita Miller-Verghy
Born 1 January 1865 Lasi, Romania
Died 31 December 1953 Bucharest, Romania of heart problems

Critic
Educator
Feminist
Journalist

Miller-Verghy was a sickly child growing up in Switzerland where her family moved after her father's death. He was descended from the Moldavian aristocracy.

She learned six languages as part of her classical education and received a Ph.D. from Geneva University in 1895.

She was a teacher, a playwright, translator, travel guides creator and contributor to many publications. Her topics were varied including teaching aids, weaving patterns, symbols and children's material.

She has been considered as the first female representative of modern Romanian Literature.

She managed a theater and a theater festival.

Her dedication to feminism was shown by the founding of the country's first women's association and as being a pioneer of Romanian scouting.

A truck hit her in Paris in 1924, leaving her blind, but she continued working and writing.

World War II left her in poverty and she relied on contributions from her students.

102. Alva Myrdal
Born 31 January 1902 Uppsala, Sweden
Died 1 February 1986 Danderyd, Sweden

Diplomat
Educator
Politician
Sociologist
Writer

All during Myrdal's career, she worked for society's betterment, emphasizing education, childcare, disarmament and peace. She led the Swedish Welfare State development.

Her *Crisis in the Population Question*, which she co-wrote, discussed social reforms for a more just society between men and women.

Her book *Urban Children* suggested reforms for preschools for all social classes. She co-founded and directed the National Education Seminar.

After World War II, she worked on welfare policy with UNESCO. Following her election to the *Riksdag*, she became the Swedish delegate to the UN disarmament conference in Geneva (1962-1973).

Her peace efforts included helping found the Stockholm International Peace Research Institute, becoming its first chairman in 1966. In 1967 she was also named consultative Cabinet minister for disarmament. Myrdal also wrote the acclaimed book *The Game of Disarmament*, originally published in 1976. A vocal supporter of disarmament.

Myrdal chaired Federation of Business and Professional Women.

103. Florence Nwanzuruahu Nkiru Nwapa

Born 13 January 1931 Uguta, Nigeria
Died 16 October 1993 Enugu, Nigeria of pneumonia

Educator
Publisher
Writer

Nwapa is called the mother of modern African Literature. She was the first to be published in English and wrote from a tribal woman's point of view to educate others about the role of women in all aspects of life.

Her degrees were from University College Ibadan and Edinburgh University.

After the Biafran War (1967-1970) she worked with the government to help orphans and refugees.

Throughout her life she worked within education as a teacher and within governmental education service, leading to cabinet posts as Ministers of Health and Social Welfare in East Central State and of Lands, Survey and Urban Development.

She published four novels, children's books and a collection of short stories. She formed Tana Press for her books and those of other writers with the goal to inform and educate women all over the world, especially Feminists (both with capital F and small f) about the role of women in Nigeria, their economic independence, their relationship with their husbands and children, their traditional beliefs and their status in the community as a whole.

104. Savitribai Phule
Born 3 January 1831 Bombay, India
Died 10 March 1897 Bombay, India of the plague

Educator
Poet
Social reformer

Phule was illiterate when she married Jyotirao Phule at age 13. Her husband home schooled her. Encouraged by friends, she attended two teacher training programs. She and her husband opened a school based on a traditional western curriculum followed by two other schools. The combined schools had 150 pupils.

The couple met with opposition from conservatives because their methods were far different from government schools. Phule carried extra saris when she traveled because she was often attacked not verbally but with rocks and dung. Her father-in-law asked the couple to leave his home where they lived because he considered their teachings sinful.

The couple set up two educational trusts. Phule is remembered for fighting for women's rights and for abolishing caste and gender discrimination.

She was a poet.

105. Anne Scheiber
Born 1 October 1893 Brooklyn, New York
Died 9 January 1995 New York, New York

Auditor
Investor
Law School Graduate

Scheiber was an ordinary auditor, but when she died, she had amassed a $22 million fortune. Her fortune went to Yeshiva University's Stern College for Women and the Albert Einstein College of Medicine. She wanted to help educate young women.

Shreiber never earned more than $3,150 a year as an IRS auditor. She was never promoted, despite being a law school graduate. It is speculated she was overlooked because she was a woman and Jewish.

How did she do it?

Being frugal and having interest-generated savings which she invested. She was said to live in the same small flat and wear the same clothes year after year, allowing her to save 80% of her salary.

It was not luck. She studied the markets and made wise decisions. She bought and held the stocks.

In the ten years between 1944 and 1945, her $20,000 quadrupled as did her annual dividends. By 1995 her $22 million portfolio was earning an annual dividend of $160,700.

106. Eve Kosofsky Sedgwick
Born 2 May 1950 Dayton, Ohio
Died 12 April 2009 New York, New York of cancer

Educator
Scholar
Writer

Sedgwick created the phrases "homosocial" and "antihomophobic." She became a warrior in the study of gender, queer theory and critical theory that are part of the culture wars.

As early as junior high in Bethesda, Maryland and despite her shyness, she participated in activities where she had to make a speech minutes after learning the subject.

She went to Radcliffe (Harvard) and later Amherst. She also taught at Hamilton, Duke, City University of New York. Her Ph.D. was from Yale.

Although she was on a tenure track at Boston University, the right-wing president's actions led to a strike: she left the university.

She found it difficult to find time for her writing, which included poetry. She moved to Berkeley where she had a reduced lecture schedule.

Her writings include *Between Men: English Literature and Male Homosocial Desire* (1985) and *Epistemology of the Closet* (1990).

Even as a gay woman, she was married happily to a man for forty years.

107. Hilda Taba
Born 7 December 1902 Kooraste, Estonia
Died 6 July 1967 San Francisco, California

Architect
Curriculum Theorist and Reformer
Educator

Her philosophy of teaching believed in:
- Concept development
- Interpretation of data
- Application of generalizations
- Interpretations of feelings, attitudes and values

Her first degree was in English and philosophy from the Tartu University, which turned her down for a job after she graduated because she was a woman.

She later went to study at Bryn Mawr College and Columbia University.

San Francisco State College hired her as a professor when she completed her Masters.

During her career she wrote seven books on the best ways to teach children.

Her belief was that learning should make students think rather than force-feed them facts.

She thought that a teacher's body language was important in encouraging or discouraging. Equally important was for the teacher not to judge the student.

Her belief in democracy was unwavering.

108. Clotilde Tambroni
Born 29 June 1758 Bologna, Italy
Died 2 June 1817 Bologna, Italy

Linguist
Philologist
Poet
Professor

Long before women could go to university, Tambroni was a Greek and literature professor at the Bologna University. She held the Greek chair. She accomplished this acceptance without having a formal university degree.

She was fluent in English, French and Spanish as well as Italian.

Using the pseudonym Doriclea Sicionia, she was part of the *Accademia degli Inestricati,* and the *Accademia degli Arcadi,* an Italian literary Academy founded in 1690.

She went to Spain to work as a researcher after she lost her Bologna University post for not swearing allegiance to the Cisalpine government, which existed in Northern Italy 1797-1799.

She was reinstated in Italy to her post and received a pay raise in 1804. Her post was later eliminated by the Napoleonic government who felt science was more important than literature.

109. Martha Carey Thomas
Born 2 January 1857 Baltimore, Maryland
Died December 1935 Philadelphia, Pennsylvania of a coronary occlusion

Educator
Linguist
Suffragist

Thomas often ran into men trying to block what she wanted.

When she was seven, the dress she wore caught fire in a cooking accident. Her mother, an ardent feminist, despite her father's doubts, cared for her and influenced her.

Although raised as a Quaker, travel in Europe made her question some of the beliefs.

Thomas had to fight her father to be allowed to attend Sage College, part of Cornell University. She then did graduate work in Greek at John Hopkins.

She went to Leipzig University, which would not allow her to graduate. At Zurich University she earned a Ph.D. in linguistics. Her dissertation on *Sir Gawain and the Green Knight* was admired for decades after.

Her first application to be president of Bryn Mawr College failed, but in 1894 she was made woman president, but was not given a ceremony. She remained president until 1908.

110. Laura Matilda Towne
Born 3 May 1825 Pittsburgh, Pennsylvania
Died 22 February1901 St. Helena Island, South Carolina of influenza

Abolitionist
Educator

Towne began her professional life by studying medicine and homeopathy.

After listening to sermons at the Philadelphia First Unitarian Church about abolition, she volunteered to teach, nurse and otherwise support freed slaves. Her family had shown interest in the cause when they lived in Boston before moving to Philadelphia.

She, and a Quaker friend Ellen Murray, founded the Penn Center, the first school to educate African Americans. Their owners had fled the area leaving some 10,000 slaves behind. The women also distributed clothing and other needed items to the freed slaves.

Towne, who had a modest inheritance, donated her time.

The center began with nine students. Murray and Towne spent forty years at the school. In later years the center became a place that taught non-violent civil disobedience.

Towne's letters and diaries were published and are available today.

111. Emma Hart Willard
Born 23 February 1787 Berlin, Connecticut
Died 15 April 1870.Troy, New York

Educator

When Willard wrote *A Plan for Improving Female Education* in 1819, many New York legislators voiced that women's education was against God's will. She rejected the idea that there were "men's subjects" and "women's subjects."

Her attitudes came from her childhood. Her father encouraged her to participate in discussions of "men's subjects."

Willard's second attempt to open a female seminary in Troy, New York succeeded after an earlier one failed. It was the first school to offer women higher education. By 1831, 300 women students were learning geography, history, philosophy and science.

However, she didn't support women voting, claimed that women were "not the satellites of men."

Her books included: *History of the United States, or Republic of America* (1828), *A System of Fulfillment of a Promise* (1831), *A Treatise on the Motive Powers which Produce the Circulation of the Blood* (1846), *Guide to the Temple of Time and Universal History for Schools* (1849) and *Last Leaves of American History* (1849).

ENGINEERS

Today, engineering is still a male-dominated profession according to research done by the Society of Women Engineers. They also earn 10% less. According to Yale Scientific, 20.9% of engineering undergraduate degrees were awarded to women.

112. Yvonne Madelaine Brill

Born 30 December 1924 Winnipeg, Manitoba, Canada
Died 27 March 2013 Princeton, NJ of breast cancer

Engineer
Inventor

Despite being a brilliant engineer one of the first comments in her *New York Times* obituary was her wonderful beef stroganoff. Her professional specialty was in rocket and jet propulsion, and she worked at NASA and the International Maritime Satellite Organization.

Early advice against trying for a career in science and opening a shop did not discourage her. Instead, she thought of her heroine Amelia Earhart.

Her dual degree in chemistry and mathematics was from Manitoba University.

Because of denial into Manitoba's school of engineering, she became a proponent of women in engineering. After her marriage to William Brill, she worked part-time to care for their three children.

At Douglas Aircraft she worked with rockets, the only female in the 1940s to do so. Her Patent No. 3,807,657 was for a new rocket engine. One of her inventions generated millions of dollars for commercial communications satellite owners.

113. Edith Clarke

Born 10 February 1883 Howard County, Maryland
Died 29 October 1959 Olney, Maryland

Engineer
Inventor
Teacher

Visitors to the Hoover Dam have no idea that a woman, Edith Clark, contributed to its design and building.

Edith Clarke had difficulty reading but excelled at mathematics. An inheritance allowed her to study at Vassar, Wisconsin University Madison, Columbia and M.I.T., where she was the first woman to earn an engineering degree.

Engineering jobs for a woman were hard to find, but she taught in Texas and Turkey.

She found work with General Electric as a computer supervisor in the Turbine Engineering Department. While there, she invented the Clarke calculator that solved line equations faster than existing methods.

Clarke achieved another gender milestone when she presented a paper at an American Institute of Electrical Engineers annual meeting.

She authored a textbook used for many years in engineering schools, as well as writing award-winning papers in 1932 and 1941.

The last ten years of her career was spent teaching at Texas University.

114. Mary Winston Jackson
Born 9 April 1921 Hampton, Virginia
Died 11 February 2005 Hampton, Virginia

Aerospace Engineer
Mathematician

Jackson was the first black female engineer at NASA. Later, she took a demotion as NASA's most senior engineer to manage the NASA Office of Equal Opportunity Programs and of the Affirmative Action Program because there she could influence the hiring and promotion of women working with NASA in science, engineering and mathematics.

Jackson held degrees in mathematics and physical science from Hampton University.

Working with children and young people was of life-long importance to her:
- She taught math at a segregated high school
- She was a Girl Scout leader
- She helped local African American children create a miniature wind tunnel to test airplanes
- She tutored high school and college students

She held some challenging assignments, working up from a research mathematician at the Langley Research Center in a still segregated department.

Jackson helped develop a wind tunnel model in 1977.

She authored or co-authored 12 technical papers.

115. Elizabeth Muriel Gregory "Elsie" MacGill
Born 27 March 1905 Vancouver, British Columbia, Canada
Died 4 November 1980 Cambridge, Massachusetts

Engineer

"Although I never learned to fly myself, I accompanied the pilots on all test flights – even the dangerous first flight – of any aircraft I worked on," Mac Gill specialized in firsts:
- First woman to earn an aeronautical engineering degree
- First Canadian woman to receive an electrical engineering degree
- First woman elected to the Engineering Institute of Canada's corporate membership
- First women to hold the position of chief engineer

She was the daughter of accomplished parents, a lawyer and judge. As a child, Jackson loved to fix things.

Although she entered the British Columbia University School of Applied Engineering, she was asked to leave after the first term. She continued her education at Toronto University.

Summers she worked in machine shops.

After a bout of polio her last year she was told she would be wheelchair bound for the rest of her life. She refused the diagnosis and walked with metal canes.

She made significant contributions to airplane design in World War II.

116. Virginia Tower Norwood
Born 8 January 1927, Queens, New York, New York
Died 26 March 2023, Los Angeles, California

Engineer
Physicist

Not every nine-year-old would be happy to be given a slide rule. Norwood was thrilled. Her father, a physicist, and her mother, a mathematician, encouraged her interest in math and physics unlike the school guidance counsellor that recommended she become a librarian.

She attended M.I.T. on scholarship.

Finding a job wasn't easy:

- One potential employer told her that they wouldn't pay what a man would get.
- Another, after she made a suggestion, told her it was brilliant, but he'd find a man to do the job.
- A third said she needed to promise not to get pregnant.

Her first job was the United States Army Signal Corps where she worked on weather radar. Later, at Hughes Aircraft, where she spent 36 years, she worked on antenna design, optics, communications links, and Landsat scanners, which earned her the description as the "Mother of Landsat" in a NASA publication. The Landsat maps the earth from space.

117. Beatrice Shilling
Born 8 March 1909 Waterlooville, Hampshire, England
Died 18 November 1990

Aeronautical Engineer
Motorcycle Racer
Sports Car Racer

Her interest in tools started as a child. At age 14 she took a motorcycle apart then put it back together.

After secondary school she worked for an electrical engineering company where the owner encouraged her to study engineering at Victory University. Her next degree was in mechanical engineering.

Her design of a device stopped Rolls Royce airplane engines from losing power during certain maneuvers. Other projects included working on airplane braking problems on wet runways and bobsled design from an Olympic team.

The Royal Aircraft Establishment (RAE) recruited her to work in publications, but in 1939 she transferred to working with aircraft engines.

She was an ardent motorcycle racer often racing on a Norton motorbike which she had modified. Along with her husband George Naylor, a World War II bomber pilot, she raced cars.

Throughout her life she experienced some discrimination including being forbidden to enter a RAE mess hall.

ENVIRONMENTALISTS

A major concern today is the environment and climate change. Fighting for the environment in many places can be dangerous and has cost some women their lives.

118. Blanca Jeannette Kawas Fernández
Born 16 January 1946 Tela Honduras
Murdered 6 February 1995 Tela Honduras

Environmental Activist

Starting her career as a certified public accountant and working in financial institutions, no one who knew her could have predicted that Kawas would be responsible for saving over 400 species of flora and fauna.

After marrying Jim Watt, with whom she had two children, she moved to New Orleans.

She continued to study and increase her professional credentials before going to work for the Honduran Ecology Association.

Her work helped save not just plants but their environment.

On 6 February 1995, back in Honduras, she was shot and killed in her home. The Hondurans let the case drop. Two local groups petitioned the Inter-American Court of Human Rights. In 2005, it found the Honduras government and two individuals responsible for the murder, setting a precedent that governments must protect environmental rights defenders.

A national Park covering 781 square meters was renamed the

Parque Nacional Jeanette Kawas.

119. Judith Arundell Wright
Born 31 May 1915 Armidale, New South Wales, Australia
Died 25 June 2000 Canberra, Australia

Activist Aboriginal Land Rights
Environmentalist
Poet
Writer

Wright was one of the early campaigners for the conservation of the
Great Barrier Reef and Fraser Island. With friends, she helped found
one of the earliest nature conservation movements.

Many of her opinions were in a posthumous book *With Love
and Fury*, a collection of selected letters with Prime Minister John
Howard.

She was equally concerned about Aboriginal land rights. In her 80s
she joined a march for their rights.

She used her pen to promote an awareness of the environment,
detailing the relationships between the different Australian groups as
well as drawing on the environment for many of her images.

Her collection of short stories included: *The Ant-lion, Eighty Acres*
and *The Weeping Fig*.

Her book, *Birds*, uses poetry to emphasize the damage being done
to the world. Again, using the power of words, she published in 1996
Earth Poems: Poems from Around the World to Honor the Earth.

From 1992, she was completely deaf.

FEMINISTS

Feminism broke into American society's consciousness as a movement in 1963 with Betty Friedan's *The Feminine Mystique*, followed by thousands of others who changed the male/female relationships at home, work and other aspects of life. But throughout history there were women who did not accept the boundaries society placed upon them as women without using the term.

120. Shulamith Bath Shmuel Ben Ari Firestone
Born 7 January 1945 Ottawa, Canada
Died 28 August 2012 New York, New York

Radical Feminist
Writer

She earned her nicknames Firebrand and Fireball, not because of her real name(s) Feuerstein and/or Firestone. It was what she did. She founded three radical feminist groups: New York Radical Women, Redstockings, and New York Radical Feminists.

She picketed a Miss America contest, set up a mock funeral for traditional womanhood and spoke out regularly on issues affecting women.

She wrote *The Dialectic of Sex: The Case for Feminist Revolution*. The book became an influential feminist text.

Her short stories included her experience with schizophrenia.

Her Orthodox Jew father's strictness planted the seeds of her rebellion. That she resented making her brother's bed just because she was a girl is just one example.

The Redstockings pushed the concept of consciousness raising to look at patriarchy against their personal lives.

121. Huda Sha'arawi or Hoda Sha'rawi
Born 23 June 1879 Minya, Egypt
Died 12 December 1947 Cairo, Egypt

Egyptian Feminist Leader
Suffragist
Nationalist

After returning from the International Woman Suffrage Alliance Congress in Rome, Sha'arawi removed her veil and mantle. Women who came to greet her were shocked at first then broke into applause: some of them removed their veils and mantles.

Within a decade of Huda's act of defiance, all Egyptian women stopped wearing veils and mantles for many decades until a retrograde movement occurred. Her decision was part of a greater movement of women and was influenced by French-born Egyptian feminist Eugénie Le Brun, but it contrasted with some feminist thinkers like Malak Hifni Nasif.

In 1923, Sha`arawi founded and became the first president of the Egyptian Feminist Union. Characteristic of liberal feminism in the early twentieth century, the EFU sought to reform laws restricting personal freedoms, such as marriage, divorce, and child custody.

She was said to suffer from paranoid schizophrenia. There have been various reasons give for her death, including starvation.

122. Kalliroe Parren
Born c 1861 Rethymno, Crete
Died 15 January 1940 Athens, Greece

Educator
Feminist
Journalist
Writer

Parren was said to have started Greece's feminist movement, but she opposed Greek involvement in World War I.

Raised in a middle-class family, she was well educated and spoke English, Greek, French, Italian and Russian.

She moved to Athens, where she ran a girls' Greek community school with her husband, a French journalist.

In 1887, she founded a woman-run newspaper *Ephemeris ton kyrion* (*Ladies' Journal*) which ran until 1916 when she was exiled for her support of the monarchy. The paper published many famous female writers.

She reached out and worked with European and American feminists. Her concentration was on education and employment for women.

Her efforts helped found *Ethniko Symvoulio ton Ellinidon* (National Council of Greek Women) affiliated with the International Council of Women.

She was willing to go to the top, contacting Theodore Deligiannis, Greek Prime Minister, who was later assassinated. Her causes included founding Sunday School, Asylum of Sainte Catherine and The Soup Kitchen. She worked to improve child protection and women's working conditions.

FILM / THEATER DIRECTORS

The percentage of women film directors in the U.S. went from 4.1% in 2011 to 14.6 in 2022 according to Stastista. In the 20th century it was even smaller. A list of current film directors can be found at https://www.studiobinder.com/blog/best-female-directors Two women directors have won the Oscar, four have been nominated. Of the 16 theater Broadway presentations (plays and musicals), women directed five that premiered on Broadway in the 2019-2020 season, three plays and two musicals.

According to the BBC's list of the 100 greatest foreign-language films, four were directed by women.

123. Vivica Aina Fanny Bandler
Born 5 February 1917 Helsinki, Finland
Died 30 July 2004 Helsinki, Finland

Agronomist
Theatre Director

Her father wanted her to be an agronomist. Her passion was for the theater, but she did agricultural studies.

Bandler started work with amateur theater in Tammela before going to Paris to study under a French movie director. Opportunities for women film directors in Finland were limited. She continued with her agricultural studies but formed a student theatre.

She bought a theatre. Her first professional production was by Jean-Paul Sartre.

Her theater work became international with productions in Norway, Sweden and France.

It was said she needed to adapt her personal style to the countries she was working in. The Finnish formality did not sit well in Sweden, for example.

Although she had a 20-year marriage with Austrian economist Kurt Bandler, she is more known for her passionate love affair with Tove Jansson, chronicled in letters. Jansson was a painter, writer and comic strip illustrator. The two women's relationship included artistic collaboration while she remained friends with Bandler.

124. Larissa Shepitko

Born 6 January 1938 Artemovsk, Ukrainian
Died 2 July 1979 Kalinin Oblast, Russian Soviet Union killed in a car accident

Film Director

The board of Gerasimov Institute of Cinematography wanted Shepitko to study acting. She insisted on directing and graduated in 1963.

She faced a major challenge to make *Heat* while suffering from hepatitis A, often directing from a stretcher.

Elem Klimov, her future husband, another student, helped her. *Heat* won the Symposium Grand Prix, the first of many recognitions for her films.

She separated herself from male directors.

Shepitko's major themes include war, a reaction to her military father. Other subjects included a female pilot, the October Revolution, an engineer bringing electricity to a village, a musical fantasy and two male surgeons.

Some films created controversy and censorship. Her last film, *The*

Ascent, won the 27th Berlin International Film Festival's Golden Bear. She was the second woman to win this award.

Her motto was the same as her teacher's at VGIK, Alexander Dovzhenko:"Make every film as if it is your last."

GEOGRAPHER

Geography as a study goes back to ancient 9th century Babylonia. It is an attempt to describe the world spatially in its simplest forms. Geographers often work in academia or government departments. There is a Society of Women Geographers with global outreach, founded in 1932.

According to the International Studies Association, feminist geography is the study of "situated knowledges derived from the lives and experiences of women in different social and geographic locations."

125. Ellen Churchill Semple

Born 8 January 1863 Louisville, Kentucky
Died 8 May 1932 West Palm Beach, Florida

Geographer

Semple wanted to study with Friedrich Ratzel, a German geographer, at Leipzig University. As a woman, she couldn't enroll but was allowed to sit in on his lectures and found herself the only woman among 500 men.

Her earlier studies included a Masters from Vassar. Her work centered on:

- Human geography
- Anthropogeography
- Environmental determinism

She became a pioneer in American geography. Her milestones

included being:

- Founding member of the Association of American Geographers (AAG)
- First and only one of six women presidents of AGA
- First faculty member, Clark University, but at a lower salary than a man

Semple was a pioneer in American geography adding human aspects of geography. Her views were documented in her two books:

- *American History and its Geographic Conditions*
- *Influences of Geographic Environment*

HISTORIANS

History is a study of the past using documents and other available information. So much of the distant past has to be gleaned from limited information, but different viewpoints of the same things can confuse the past. The discovery of a diary, for example, can solve what some person believed, changing everything known about an event. Current beliefs can influence how the past was considered. Currently in the U.S. women historians outnumber men, according to www.zippia.com 59.3% to 40.7% in 2023. The pay gap is tiny, 99 cents for every dollar.

126. Bertha Eckstein-Diener
Born 18 March 1874 Vienna, Austria
Died 20 February 1948 Geneva, Switzerland after surgery

Historian
Intellectual
Mountaineer
Skater
Skier
Translator
Travel Journalist
Writer

Known as Sir Galahad in her 1930 intellectual group called the "Arthurians," she was determined to document feminist history. Other members took Arthur's Round Table names.

Her book *Mothers and Amazons* is considered a classic of matriarchal history. She wrote other books under the Sir Galahad name.

She was also known by the names Helen Diner and Ahasvera (perpetual traveler).

She grew up in Vienna and was from a middle-class family. She was known as an excellent figure skater and later became a skier and was a mountaineer.

She married Austrian scholar Friedrich Eckstrain but left him and her first son to travel in Egypt, England and Greece. She had a second son in 1910 by Theodore Beer. Her maternal urges were probably minor. She placed the boy with a foster family. They reunited twice, once in 1936 and 1938.

Besides books she wrote for newspapers and translated three American journalists' work.

127. Mary Anne Everett Green
Born 19 July 1818 Sheffield, England
Died 1 November 1895 London, England

Archivist
Historian
Writer

When entering an archive few people wonder who established it. Green was a force behind the English national archive.

She was another woman whose father insisted she have in-depth education.

The British Museum was her hunting ground. With her language skills she was able to write the multi-volume *Letters of Royal and Illustrious Ladies* (1846) and *Lives of the Princesses of England: from the Norman Conquest* (1849–1855). She wrote summaries of state papers, organizing them in chronological order.

Unlike men working on the same projects, she had no paid assistant. Her sister helped her.

She argued over her lower pay as well as ideas to improve the archive.

As a woman, she was often confined to working on papers from other women. She wrote 700 pages of prefaces to seventh-century documents and edited 41 volumes of papers.

Her methods, however, set a standard for research.

128. Ragnhild Hatton
Born 10 January 1913 Bergen, Norway
Died 16 May 1995 London, England

Historian

She was called a glutton for footnotes.

She and her businessman husband moved from Norway to London, where she continued her studies. World War II and her two sons' births interrupted her career, but in 1947 she received her Ph.D. from University College.

Her career centered around academia. She worked her way up from assistant lecturer, lecturer, reader, to a professor of international history at the London School of Economics.

She was also:

- Dean of the Faculty of Economics and Political Science
- Chairman of the History Department, LSE
- London Honours Board of Examiners in History
- External examiner in history for Nottingham, Edinburgh University, Queens and Warwick Universities
- Royal Historical Society Council member

She was fluent in several European languages.

Her publications earned her the title of Britain's leading 17th and

18th century historian. International recognition included Fellow of the Swedish *Vitterhetsakademie* and the first foreign woman historian of the American Historical Association.

129. Grace Raymond Hebard
Born 2 July 1861 Clinton, Ohio
Died 11 October 1936 Laramie, Wyoming

Educator
Engineering Graduate
Historian
Lawyer
Political Economist
Suffragist
Writer

Hebard's research took her walking through Wyoming's mountains and plains to talk to people for their stories. She published many of her findings. Sometimes, those reports have been questioned as to their authenticity.

Although she was home educated, she did well at university and earned degrees from Iowa University and Illinois Wesleyan University in person and by correspondence. Her enrollment in the engineering department at Iowa brought predictions she would fail.

She didn't.

She was the first woman on the Wyoming State Bar Association.

Active politically, she was a:
- Suffragist
- Lobbyist for child-welfare laws
- Red Cross volunteer
- Sold war bonds
- Organized immigrant classes

She became a force at Wyoming University as a professor and a member of the Board of Trustees occupying herself with much of the development of the university. She taught a variety of courses including law, banking, sociology, labor relations and more.

She was described by the WyoHistoryOrg as a "Wyoming renaissance woman."

130. Lucy Myers Wright Mitchell
Born 20 March 1845 Urumiah, Persia (Iran)
Died 10 March 1888 Lausanne, Switzerland after a fall

Archeologist
Historian
Writer

Mitchell "caught" her love of archeology from her father, Austin Wright, a medical missionary to Iran. Like many women of her time, her education, after being sent to stay with family in Andover, Massachusetts, was formal and informal depending on time and place.

Her studies at Mount Holyoke College were cut short when she accompanied her father to Persia. The stay was shortened when he died.

After marrying Samuel Mitchell, the couple moved to Europe, allowing her to explore archeological sites as well as integrate with artistic and academic groups.

Her interest in art history grew with her research, leading to her giving a series of lectures.

The American Ambassador to Rome suggested she write a book on ancient sculpture. The work covered 700 pages of documentation and text with an extensive bibliography.

Her combination of detail, ancient written sources and recent archeological discoveries made experts take the work seriously.

She was planning a second book on Greek vases, when she fell ill and died.

131. Linda Nochlin
Born 30 January 1931 New York, New York
Died 29 October 2017 Manhattan, New York

Art Historian
Feminist
Writer

Why Have There Been No Great Women Artists? Nochlin wrote a book asking just that. Much of her life was spent dealing with the question. She wanted to know how gender affects art both from the point of view of the creator and the viewer. Growing up in Brooklyn gave her the opportunity to visit some great art museums.

She held a B.S. from Vassar and earned a Ph.D. in art history in 1963 from the Institute of Fine Arts at New York University.

Before teaching at the Institute of Fine Arts the remainder of her professional life, she taught at Yale, City University of New York and Vassar.

In 1976 and 2007 she was co-curator of two exhibitions that featured women artists. The 2007 exhibition was the first dedicated to 88 women artists. The 1976 Women Artists: 1550-1950 featured 83 artists from 12 countries.

INTELLIGENCE OFFICERS / SPIES

Intelligence officers, which is not a rank but a designation, gather information. During the two world wars many women worked with men or by themselves to spy on the activities of the enemy for their governments. Many were captured and did not survive. Spies risked their lives.

132. Etta Lubina Johanna Palm d'Aelders
Born April 1743 Groningen, Netherlands
Died 28 March 1799 Netherlands

Feminist
Spy

She was a Dutch spy who changed sides when it was in her interest and a committed feminist.

Born into a middle-class family, her mother saw that she received an education superior to women of her time and class.

She spoke to the French National Convention in 1790: *The Injustice of the Laws in Favour of Men, at the Expense of Women.*

She founded the *Société patriotique et de bienfaisance des Amies de la Vérité.*

D'Aelders used these political platforms to instruct French citizens on the struggles of women and to show men the harm that was being caused to the lives of women hampered by social inferiority.

Who recruited her as a spy for the French Secret Service is not known. She also spied for The Netherlands and Prussia. She used her contacts to try to influence the 1795 Treaty of Hague.

D'Aelders was arrested and imprisoned in the Woerden fortress. When released she was in fragile health and died a few months later.

133. Inayat Khan aka Nora Baker
Born 1 January 1914 Moscow, Russia
Executed 13 September 1944 Bavaria, Germany

Spy
Writer

Baker was a pacifist turned spy.

In World War II she served under the code name Madeleine for the Special Operations Executive (SOE) whose mission was to spy and commit sabotage in Nazi-occupied countries.

She trained as a wireless operator. Their survival rates were considered between six weeks and two months. Operators looked for places to set up and hide equipment. More than 20 minutes of transmission risked being detected.

At one point she was the only surviving wireless operator in the region.

The person who betrayed her to the Gestapo was never discovered, but they arrested Baker in October 1943 and took her to 84 Avenue Foch, the Nazi center of counterintelligence. She escaped once but was recaptured. Then they sent her to Dachau where she was executed with three other women.

134. Virginia Hall Goillot
Born 6 April 1906 Baltimore, Maryland
Died 8 July 1982 Rockville, Maryland

Spy

Not many women have code names. Goillot had many including Marie and Diane. The Germans nicknamed her Artemis. The Gestapo called her the most dangerous of all Allied spies. Other names were Limping Lady and Mayor of Lyon.

Not every spy has a prothesis leg named Cuthbert.

During World War II, Goillot worked with Britain's Special Operations Executive (SOE) and the American Office of Strategic Services (OSS) in France against the occupying Nazis beginning in August 1941.

She formed a network that supplied agents with the tools they needed to gather information and get downed pilots to safety. Later she was a wireless operator and supplied arms and training to French resistance groups like the *Maquis.*

Her experience would make an adventure series. At one point she walked 50 miles from Perpignan to Spain over mountainous territory. She disguised herself as an old woman.

After the war, she became one of the first women to work for the CIA. Despite her accomplishments she faced discrimination and was described as "a woman of no importance."

135. Kitty Harris
Born: 24 May 1902 London, Ontario, Canada
Died 1966 Gorky, Russia

Factory Worker
Seamstress
Spy

Under the code name Ada/Aida, Harris was courier for the OGPU-NKVD (Russian police).

Daughter of a poor Polish immigrant shoemaker, her first job was in a factory. She helped lead a 1919 strike of the Industrial Workers of the World.

Although formally uneducated, she spoke several languages.

In January 1923 she joined the USA Communist Party: in 1927 she transferred to the Russian Communist party and became Russian in 1927.

Her training in cryptography, photography and radio was in Moscow in 1936 before she went to London. Later she was based in Paris until the city fell to the Nazis and she moved to Moscow.

She worked out of Berlin, Los Alamos, Los Angeles, Mexico, New York and Paris, where she lived as the alleged wife of the Russian ambassador during World War II.

She served as a courier in China, the lover of a British diplomat and as a spy on the Manhattan project.

In Santa Fe, NM she ran a safe house in a drug store in the early 1940s.

136. Gabrielle Maria Petit
Born 20 February 1893 Tournai, Belgium
Executed 1 April 1916 Brussels, Belgium

Nanny
Saleswoman
Spy

Using false names and identities, Petit fed information about the German Army to British intelligence during World War I while keeping notes on cigarette papers that she could burn if caught.

Born to a poor family, Petit was put in the Sisters of the Child Jesus orphanage after her mother's death from surgery. There she was required to do cleaning chores.

When her fiancé was wounded in the war, she quit her sales job to join the Belgian Red Cross. She helped him rejoin his unit by smuggling him across The Netherlands border. He would be the first of many that she would help make the trip.

During the trip, she noticed the German Army's position and she gave that information to the British intelligence. They, in turn, hired her as a spy.

She was a distributor of *La Libre Belgique* and the underground mail service until the German intelligence caught up with her.

She was shot after refusing to give the Germans information.

137. Agnes Smedley
Born 23 February 1892 Osgood, Missouri
Died 6 May 1950 London UK after ulcer surgery

Journalist
Spy
Writer

Smedley has been called one of the most prolific female spies of the 20th century. She was a triple agent for the Soviets, Chinese Communists and Indian nationalists. The people she met at New York University in 1912 created the connections that helped her as a spy.

She worked with the Friends of Freedom for India keeping their documents from the government. She was arrested and indicted but not tried.

She taught at Berlin University and founded a birth control clinic.

She spied on the British in Shanghai. She found a lover, who was executed in 1944. He claimed she helped him using her code name.

When she worked for a U.S. general, she encouraged him to send supplies to Chinese Communists.

The U.S. Government became suspicious and began monitoring her activity. She was subpoenaed to appear before the House Un-American Activities Committee, but she had moved to England.

She wrote *Daughter of Earth*, an autobiographical novel.

138. Diana Ruth Wellesley, Duchess of Wellington
Born 14 January 1922 London, England
Died 1 November 2010 London, England

Intelligence Officer World War II

Wellesley, in the role as a military secretary/intelligence officer in Jerusalem, discovered that the Stern Gang, dedicated to evicting the British from Israel, was planning to bomb the church where she was to marry Valerian Wellesley, future 9th Duke of Wellington.

Passing on top secret documents was part of her regular duties. She also handled documents about the plans for a British invasion of Iraq.

The bomb was discovered: the wedding went ahead.

Although she was from a military family (her father was Major-General Douglas McConnel) she promised herself not to marry a military man. It was a promise she broke. Her husband was a military man and the wedding had been rushed because of his posting to Italy.

INVENTORS

If some of the women described below had not existed, women might still be washing dishes by hand, ironing a lot more and struggling to see when driving in the rain.

139. Mary Elizabeth Anderson
Born 19 February 1866 Green County, Alabama
Died 27 June 1953 Monteagle, Tennessee

Inventor
Rancher
Real Estate Developer
Viticulturist

When you are driving in the rain, and put on your windshield wipers, thank Mary Anderson, who invented the first one, which was hand operated. The idea came when she was riding on a New York trolley and the driver was having trouble seeing through the sleet-covered windshield.

On 10 November 1903, she received patent number 743,80. When she tried to sell her patent, she was unsuccessful: it was considered to have little commercial value. Cadillac was the first car manufacturer to adopt wipers in 1922, two years after her patent expired. She never earned any money for it.

A second woman, Charlotte Bridgewood, invented an electric windshield wiper, but like Anderson never received any money.

Anderson's great niece said explaining why her aunt was never paid,

"She didn't have a father. She didn't have a husband. And the world was kind of run by men back then."

The lack of a male protector did not stop her from developing real estate and running a cattle range.

140. Ruth Mary Rogan Benerito
Born 12 January 1916 New Orleans, Louisiana
Died 5 October 2013 Metairie, Louisiana

Chemist
Inventor

The need to NOT iron cotton clothes is thanks to Benerito's invention of wash-and-wear cotton. She holds 55 patterns. Rather than take full credit, she said, "I don't like it to be said that I invented wash-wear because there were any number of people who worked on it and the various processes by which you give cotton those properties. No one person discovered it or is responsible for it, but I contributed to a new process of doing it."

Raised by pro-women's liberation parents, Benerito was encouraged to follow her interests in math and chemistry. Unlike many parents, they believed a woman's education was as important as a man's.

She studied at many universities: Bryn Mawr College, Tulane University and the University of Chicago. She often combined her research with teaching.

Her research into cotton fibers coincided with her work at the USDA Southern Regional Research Center in the 1950s.

141. Amalie Auguste Melitta Bentz
Born 31 January 1873 Dresden, Germany
Died 29 June 1950 Porta Westfallica, Germany

Entrepreneur
Inventor

Anytime a person puts a paper coffee filter in their coffee maker, it is because of Bentz, who invented the filters.

Born into a successful business family, she married a small business owner.

Annoyed that coffee percolators overflowed or left grounds and using her son's school exercise book and a brass pot, she experimented with alternatives.

She received a patent and set up a business. Her family were her first employees. Her home was the office and factory.

Sales grew until 1928 when she needed 80 employees. As they expanded more workers were needed. It had a social fund which provided bonuses and 15 vacation days.

In 1932 her sons, Willy and Horst became the head.

World War II stopped production. It was resumed in 1948.

Today the company has 3,400 employees in 50 countries. The family still owns the company.

142. Josephine Cochrane
Born 8 March 1839 Ashtabula County, Ohio
Died 3 August 1913 Chicago, Illinois of a stroke

Inventor

Anyone with a sink of dirty dishes and a dishwasher should thank Josephine Cochran. In 1886, she patented the first commercial dishwasher. She had been upset when her own china was chipped after a party during the clean-up.

Cochran felt a machine should save time without breaking dishes. She vowed, "If nobody else is going to invent a dishwashing machine, I'll do it myself." She used water pressure and fitted racks.

Men were hesitant to produce the machine until in 1886 George Butters helped her build a prototype in her shed.

The $100 price tag was a deterrent to sales. After exhibiting at the 1893 Columbian Exhibition World's Fair in Chicago, sales boomed. Five years later she opened a factory.

There were many ups and downs. Home dishwashers gained in popularity in the 1950s.

143. Caresse Crosby
Born 20 April 1892 New York, New York
Died 24 January 1970 Rome, Italy heart disease

Businesswoman
Inventor
Mother of the Lost Generation
Publisher

When you put on a bra, think of this woman who patented the modern bra. Other patents existed but hers had features similar to the bra of today. And unlike corsets, it was pliable.

Coming from a society family, she was dressing for dinner and unhappy at being forced into an uncomfortable corset. She took two handkerchiefs and some ribbon and created the comfortable bra.

Her patent was granted in November 1914, and using her first husband's funds opened a mini-manufacturing unit with two seamstresses. It was called Fashion Form Brassière.

Years later she and Harry Crosby, her second husband, lived in

Paris and founded the Black Sun Press. They identified many new writers that would become famous such as Hemingway, MacLeish and Miller.

The couple had moved to Paris from Boston, where their affair had created a scandal not just because he was seven years younger. In Paris the couple's life was filled with drugs, alcohol and affairs. Her husband shot his lover and killed himself. After his death she renamed the publisher Crosby Continental Editions.

Throughout the remainder of her life, Crosby continued to live unconventionally with affairs and marriages.

144. Beulah Louise Henry
Born 28 September 1887 Raleigh, North Carolina
Died 1 February 1973

Inventor

"I invent because I cannot help it - new things just thrust themselves on me," Henry said.

Called "Lady Edison," Henry is credited with 110 inventions and 49 patents. Unlike many inventors, she profited from some of her creations either through founding a company or advising companies who were producing her inventions.

Her inventions include a vacuum ice cream freezer, hair curler, sponge soap dish, clip on parasol in pretty colors, a bobbin-free sewing machine.

She found a way for typists to make a duplicate copy long before there were copy machines, eliminating the need for messy carbon paper.

She invented toy improvements, more for girls than boys. Stuffed animals were given joints. Dolls had movable eyes. A spinning top could replace dice in board games.

The Journal of the Patent Office Society, in 1937, described her as, "America's leading feminine inventor" the same year a museum in Osaka held an exhibition to encourage Japanese women inventors.

145. Margaret Eloise Knight
Born 14 February 1838 York, Maine
Died 12 October 1914 Framingham, Massachusetts

Inventor

Whenever you put down a paper bag and it doesn't fall over, think of Knight. She invented a machine to produce flat-bottomed paper bags and founded the Eastern Paper Bag Company in 1870.

As a child she preferred a jack knife, gimlet and wood instead of dolls. That she made kites and sleds was a precursor to her becoming an inventor.

As a young adult she worked in the Manchester, New Hampshire cotton mills. There she witnessed an accident. She invented a safety device to prevent similar accidents.

She held many different jobs, mostly working with her hands.

When Charles Annan saw an iron model of her paper bagmaker he stole the concept and patented it before Knight could. She filed a lawsuit.

Although *Smithsonian Magazine* argued no woman could have designed such a machine, she won her case and her patent when she presented evidence of the development.

146. Elizabeth J. Magie Phillips
Born 9 May 1866 Macomb, Illinois
Died 2 March 1948 Arlington, Virginia

Actress
Engineer
Feminist
Game Designer
Georgist (single tax movement)
Inventor
Journalist
Stenographer
Typist
Writer

Probably everyone has played Monopoly at one time or another. Philips invented *The Landlord's Game*, the precursor to Monopoly. Despite its capitalist leanings, she wanted it to show progressive thinking.

She was born into a family of abolitionists and publishers. Her father had traveled with Abraham Lincoln.

She patented a typewriting process improving how paper was fed and was one of the 1% of women who received a patent.

Her idea that women were as capable as men was considered radical.

Dissatisfied with the salary that she was earning, she took out a newspaper ad offering herself as a white slave.

Other versions of Monopoly, whose patent expired in 1921, had names like Br'er Fox, Br'er Rabbit. The latter was not proven to be patent protected.

Parker Brothers took over the game. Phillips never received full credit.

JOURNALISTS

According to Pew Research Center 51% of U.S. journalists are men, who are more apt to cover sports, politics, science and the economy. Women are more likely to cover health, entertainment, education and social issues. Being a journalist can be dangerous. Ninety-three journalists were killed in 2023 and 400 were imprisoned worldwide.

147. Khadijah Muhammad Abdullah Al-Jahami
Born 15 March 1921 Born Benghazi, Libya
Died 11 August 1996 Benghazi, Libya

Broadcaster
Journalist
Nurse World War II
Songwriter
Women's rights advocate, also known as "Bint Al-Watan"
Writer

As a young child, she wrote Benito Mussolini, criticizing Italian colonialism in Libya. She knew Italian because her father, poet Muhammad Abdullah al-Jahmi, sent her to school where Italian was taught as well as Arabic.

She was a nurse in World War II.

She was only the second woman broadcaster in Libya. Her programs centered on artists, children, health, women's issues and other related topics.

She founded or participated in:
- • A women's and children's magazines
- • The founding of a women's union

She became creator, publisher and editor of *Al-Bayt,* the Women's Magazine.

Libya's ex-foreign minister, Abdul Rahman Shalgam, described her as having "launched a quiet social revolution."

148. Louie Bennett
Born 7 January 1870 Dublin, Ireland
Died 25 November 1956 Dublin, Ireland

Feminist
Journalist
Pacifist
Suffragist
Trade unionist
Writer

Imagine a woman who has a stamp AND a bench on Stephen's Green in Dublin with her name on it. Louie Bennett does have one for her work fighting for women's suffrage and for workers. Yet, how many people who walk by them, know what she did, who she was.

She founded the Irish Women's Suffrage Federation in 1911.

Her first two books were romantic novels. She said she wrote them at her dressing table but hid them from others.

Her writing included being joint editor and contributor to the *Irish Citizen* newspaper and two books.

She played a significant role in the Irish Women Workers' Union (IWWU) and was the first woman president of the Irish Trade Union Congress. The emphasis of their work was equal pay for women and opportunities for jobs. A three-month strike won the right for two weeks paid vacation for all workers.

Bennett was active in leadership of the IWWU until 1955.

All her life she was a dedicated pacifist.

149. Marvel Jackson Cooke
Born 4 April 1903 Mankato, Minnesota
Died 29 November 2000 Manhattan, New York of leukemia

Civil Rights Activist
Journalist

Cooke experienced racism from a teacher and from other children when growing up in an all-white Minnesota community.

She was one of four black students out of 20,000 at Minnesota University.

Racism showed itself again when she qualified as a Spanish translator for the War Department but was only allowed to be a file clerk. Whites were translators — not blacks.

It did not stop her from a successful journalistic career working for black leaders Adam Clayton Powell and W.E.B. Dubois, who mentored her. Through them, her job reporting for the NACCP magazine *The Crisis*, she met leading black writers, artists and performers after she moved to New York during the Harlem Renaissance.

She was the first woman to work for *New York Amsterdam News*, and the first African American woman to write for a mainstream white-owned newspaper.

She actively fought for justice by supporting strikes, Angela Davis, and other related issues.

150. Natalya Khusainovna Estemirova
Born 28 February 1958 Kamyshlov, Sverdlovsk Oblast, Russia
Assassinated 15 July 2009 Gazi-Yurt, Ingushetia, Russia

Activist Human Rights
Journalist
Teacher

A woman who investigated kidnappings herself was a victim. Witnesses claimed that on 15 July 2009, they saw Estemirova shoved into a car as she yelled about being kidnapped. Her bullet-ridden body was later found. For her work she received the Swedish Right Livelihood Award and the Robert Shuman medal.

She had been gathering evidence of human rights abuses in photographs and testimony which were published in *The Voice* and *The Worker of Grozny*. Her research was the subject of 13 documentaries.

Estemirova was the widow of a Chechen policeman.

Two people, journalist Anna Politkovskaya and lawyer Stanislav Markelov, whom she worked with, were also murdered at different times.

Although Russian President Dmitry Medvedev expressed his horror at her death, the allegedly known murderer has never been prosecuted. Alkhazur Bashayev was named as a possibility, but he also was killed.

The European Court of Human Rights (ECtHR) ruled that Russian authorities have failed to properly investigate the murder.

151. Gauri Lankesh

Born 29 January 1962 Bangalore, India
Murdered 5 September 2017 Bangalore, India by being shot

Activist
Journalist

Opposing right-wing Hindu extremism and the caste system and promoting women's rights, Lankesh wrote for and edited her father's weekly, *Gauri Lankesh Patrike*. Over her career, she wrote for other newspapers.

After her father's death, she and her brother, Indrajat, shared responsibilities for their father's paper, she as writer and him handling the finances. In 2001, their ideologies were in conflict, but only became public in 2005. Her brother filed charges against her for "stealing" computer equipment.

She started *Lankesh Patrike,* her own weekly. A believer in freedom of the press, she was outspoken in the editorial policy, often attacking the powerful.

She was targeted in a defamation suit that led to her imprisonment.

Three men on motorcycles shot her seven times outside her home causing instantaneous death.

152. Camille Lepage

Born 28 January 1988 Angers, France
Murdered 12 May 2014 Central African Republic

Photojournalist

Lepage was the first murder victim during the Central African Republic conflict in 2014.

She had studied photojournalism at Southampton Solent University before freelancing in Africa, basing herself in Juba, South Sudan.

She considered she was just getting started in her work, but she found it amazing to travel to remote areas to meet people.

Her early work appeared in major U.S. French, English and Arabic media, both print and broadcast.

It bothered her that some conflicts were not covered "because no one can make money out of them."

Her decision to cover them despite warnings of the dangers would lead to her death in an area of intense fighting. French peacekeepers found her body inside a Christian militia vehicle.

153. Ella Maillart

Born 20 February 1903 Geneva, Switzerland
Died 27 March 1997 Chandolin, Switzerland

Adventurer
Journalist
Photographer
Travel Writer

No woman of her time or any time would take a 3,500-mile trip through China including desert and mountain terrains. Maillart did.

Her accomplishments included:
- Captained and organized the first Swiss women's field hockey team
- Represented Switzerland in single-handed yacht competition in the 1924 Paris Olympics
- Sailed to Crete with an all-woman crew
- Studied filmmaking in Berlin and Moscow
- Member of the Swiss ski team

She reported on the Japanese occupation in Manchuria for *Le Petit Parisien*.

Her explorations included the Muslim republics of the USSR and Asia.

Over the years she traveled by camel, foot, horse, train and truck through deserts and mountains.

She spent her last years in Switzerland.

154. Mary Margaret McBride
Born 7 April 1976 Paris, Missouri
Died 16 November 1899 West Shokan, New York

Journalist
Radio Broadcaster

Not many people will remember McBride as "The First Lady of Radio." Some may remember her as Martha Dean, the persona she adopted as a grandmother of what turned out to be imaginary grandchildren. She quickly abandoned the grandchildren, finding it too complicated to memorize all the children's details.

With a degree in journalism McBride worked for a number of newspapers and as a freelance writer for magazines like the *Saturday Evening Post, Cosmopolitan* and *Good Housekeeping.*

In 1934 she began her daily radio show dispensing advice to women in a Missouri drawl. It aired daily until 1940.

When she changed stations she worked under a new name, Bessie Beatty. There she interviewed famous people in the arts and politics.

She allowed no product to be advertised if she was not a personal user. Alcohol ads were also refused.

She co-authored several books on a variety of subjects.

155. Georgette Louise Meyer (Dickey Chapelle)
Born 14 March 1918 Milwaukee, Wisconsin
Shot 4 November1965 Quảng Ngãi province, South Vietnam from
shrapnel

Photojournalist
War Correspondent

Because she wanted to fly planes more than design them, she left her
studies at M.I.T.

After moving to Coral Gables, Florida, she found work writing
press releases for an airshow followed by an assignment in Havana,
Cuba. Her coverage of an air accident there led to a job with TWA's
publicity department.

She specialized in dangerous assignments, covering the battles of
Iwo Jima and Okinawa and the Hungarian Revolution. If she had
to jump from an airplane for an assignment, she did. At one point in
1956 she was jailed.

Fidel Castro called her, "the polite little American with all that
tiger blood in her veins."

She combined army fatigues, a bush hat and pearl earrings.

Her death came during Operation Black Ferret in Vietnam when a
piece of shrapnel cut her carotid artery.

156. Hazel Freeman Smith
Born 4 February 1914 Alabama City, Alabama
Died 15 May 1994 Cleveland, Tennessee of Alzheimer's

Journalist
Publisher

She described herself as "just a little editor in a little spot," despite being the first woman to be awarded a Pulitzer Prize for editorial writing. Other awards followed.

She had purchased four Mississippi weekly papers starting in her twenties. They were the *Durant* News, *Lexington Advertiser, Banner County Outlook* and the *Northside Reporter*. They gave her a voice, one that wasn't always popular. Hatred for her led to the firing of her husband as county hospital administrator.

She annoyed both sides on segregation. Her belief in separate but equal led to anti-segregationists fire-bombing her office. The KKK burned a cross on her lawn.

Her column *Through Hazel's Eyes* often covered unpopular causes. She would report positive stories about blacks, not just black crime stories.

She reported on a venereal disease clinic, bootlegging and gambling.

Her attitude toward the injustice was further fueled when she saw a sheriff shoot a black man in the thigh. Her editorial led to the sheriff suing for libel. His $10,000 award was overturned by the state supreme court.

LABOR LEADERS

People want to be paid fairly for the labor and safe working conditions, simple demands that have been an on-going battle through time against those who deny them those rights. The battle is still going on, but those who fought for the worker fought bravely often at great personal cost. Even those who don't belong to a labor union have benefited from their fights.

157. Agnes Nestor
Born 24 June 1880 Grand Rapids, Michigan
Died 28 December 1948 Chicago, Illinois respiratory illness

Labor Leader

Working conditions at her first job at Eisendrath Glove Company helped mold Nestor's labor views. Workers were charged rentals for the machines they used and had to buy their own needles. She helped organize a 10-day strike.

The workers won.

Nestor became an officer of the International Glove Workers Union and worked with other women's clubs of various classes.

She participated in the Women's Trade Union League (WTUL), serving all classes and wanted to unite all women to improve working conditions in terms of hours, pay and citizenship. As part of organizing a report was issued: "Exhibit of Dynamic Sweatshops."

Proposed bills failed.

The WTUL promoted women's education.

Although she lost the political jobs she ran for, she was against the Equal Rights Amendment.

After her retirement, she continued to recruit women for the labor organization and fight for labor laws.

158. Marta Matamoros
Born 17 February 1909 Panama City, Panama
Died 28 December 2005 Panama City, Panama

Communist
Dressmaker
Labor Leader
Shoemaker
Unionist

Panamanian women have paid maternity leave thanks to Matamoros.

She fought hard as the first woman General Secretary of the Trade Union Federation of Panama. That and her Communist membership made her the target of government investigations.

Her father, a musician, nationalist and humanitarian, helped form her beliefs.

The reality of no money forced her to work as a shoemaker and dressmaker where she realized how bad working conditions were: 11-13 hour days, minimal pay, small-cramped cubicles.

She joined a union and worked her way through the ranks.

In 1945 she led a strike for better working conditions. It brought the issue to public attention. Over the years, she led many other protests and served 99 days in prison for her support of a bus driver strike.

She was a delegate of the World Federation of Trade Union Congress in Vienna, Austria in 1953.

"The Hunger and Desperation March," which she led, was successful in bringing in a minimum wage law.

159. Emma Anne Paterson
Born 5 April 1848 London, England
Died 1 December 1886 Westminster, England from diabetes

Feminist
Trade Unionist

A believer in women-only labor unions, she went to work for the Nation Society for Women's Suffrage. In 1874 she founded the Women's Protective and Provident League (WPPL) and later the Women's Trade Union League (WTLU).

The concept came from her visit to the Female Umbrella Maker's Union of New York during her honeymoon with Thomas Paterson, a Scottish cabinetmaker. He shared her union views. Members were mainly from the upper middle class wishing to improve social conditions. She also encouraged the formation of a similar group in Bristol.

A woman's bookbinder's league was founded in 1874.

Paterson was the first woman to be a delegate to the Trade Union Congress in 1875 in Glasgow. In 1876 she began to edit the *Woman's Union Journal.*

After founding the Women's Printing Society, she mastered printing.

The demands of the WTLU mirrored the men's demands, added a maternity section.

160. Crystal Lee Sutton
Born 31 December 1940 Roanoke Rapids, North Carolina
Died 11 September 2009 Burlington, North Carolina of brain cancer

Labor Organizer

Many people loved Sally Field in *Norma Rae*, but few of them knew it was based on the real- life Sutton.

She was an ordinary factory-working mother who was tired, tired of working conditions, tired of low pay ($2.65 an hour). "Management and others treated me as if I had leprosy," she said.

The Amalgamated Clothing and Textile Workers Union (ACTWU) began to organize workers at a J.P. Stevens mill as well as promote a boycott of their products.

Sutton was fired when she joined the organization's attempt which went from 1963-1978, although a contract wasn't signed for two more years.

When Sutton was fired, she held up a union sign as was shown in the movie. Sutton made a speaking tour as a paid organizer for the ACTWU. She was eventually rehired by J.P. Stevens.

LAWYERS

Women had a hard time cracking the legal profession ceiling in the United States and in Europe. Even when allowed to study the law, they were not allowed to practice and even when they were, law firms were hesitant to hire them. Being a lawyer certainly did not match the male concept for ladylike comportment.

161. Edith Hahn Beer
Born 24 January 1914 Vienna, Austria
Died 17 March 2009 London, England

Holocaust survivor
Lawyer
Judge

Higher education for girls was unusual in 1914 Vienna, but Hahn's Jewish family sent her to university.

The *Anschluss* ended her education. She and her mother were sent to an asparagus farm and then to a paper factory before her mother was deported to Poland.

Hahn obtained Christian identity papers. In Munich she volunteered as a Red Cross nurse.

She married Werner Vetter, a Nazi party member. Although partially blind, he was still drafted. They had a daughter.

After the war, Hahn reclaimed her Jewish identity.

The Soviets appointed her as a judge. When she was pressured to act as a KGB informant, she escaped to London with her daughter.

There she worked as a maid and corset designer.

In 1957, she married Fred Beer, a Jewish jeweler, and they remained married until his death in 1984. After Beer's death, Hahn emigrated to Israel but returned to London.

162. Marianne Beth

Born 6 March 1889 Vienna, Austria
Died 19 August 1984 New York, New York

Lawyer
Scholar

She was one of the lucky women with a father who supported her by having her privately tutored to guarantee she received an education beyond what most women received.

After several rejections, Beth was finally able to study law. She also studied religious psychology and earned a doctorate in Orientalism.

In 1919 when women were admitted to the law school, she enrolled and became the first Austrian woman lawyer. She worked for the advancement and acceptance of other women in the legal profession.

Born into a Jewish family, she married a Christian and converted. However, when the Nazis took over Austria, her name was removed from the list of lawyers.

Before emigrating to the U.S., she spoke on women's issues and wrote a handbook, *The Right of Women* and co-founded an Austrian woman's group. She continued to speak out.

In 1935 she published *Unbelief as a manifestation of deficit.*

163. Margrith Bigler-Eggenberger
Born 14 March 1933 Uzwil St. Gallen, Switzerland
Died 5 September 2022 St. Gallen, Switzerland

Judge
Lawyer
University Lecturer

"Obviously my CV had been cut down to reflect this false image of the incompetent woman who wants to move from the stove to the Federal Supreme Court," Bigler-Eggenberger said on becoming the first woman judge on the Swiss Federal Supreme Court. When she talked about her first days as a judge, she said, "Some of my colleagues even refused to talk to me."

Her selection had been hampered by some of her documents being withheld.

She entered the court a year after Swiss women gained the right to vote, something she had supported.

Her family never thought women's rights should be any different from men's. Her family had housed Jewish refugees in World War II.

A graduate of Zurich and Geneva Universities, she was issued her lawyer's license in 1961.

Her dissertation was based on her work in detention facilities.

She became an expert in women's issues and was a member of the board of the Alliance of Women Organizations.

She fought for equal pay.

164. Bettisia Gozzadini

Born c 1209 Bologna, Italy
Died 2 November 1261 Budrio, Italy during a flood

Jurist

Many legends surround Gozzadini, who was from a noble family, including that she often dressed in men's clothing. Another legend was that she had to wear a veil or sit behind a screen when teaching, to avoid distracting her students.

She had studied philosophy and law at the Studium of Bologna which later offered her a chair. She refused it the first time, not the second.

Not only was she the first Italian woman to be granted a university degree, she could well have been the first university woman teacher. Prior to the teaching offer, she had been tutoring about 30 students in law from her home. Her classes were so popular, she often had to move them to a public square.

Because of her oration skills she spoke at the funeral of the Bishop of Bologna in May 1242.

Her early death was caused by the collapse of a house from flood waters.

165. Lidia Poët

26 August 1855 Perrero, Italy
Died 25 February 1949 Diano Marina, Italy

Lawyer

Women who want to be lawyers in Italy today benefited from Lidia Poët's disbarment.

Poët passed her law examinations after graduating from the Turin

University Law School in 1881. She completed the necessary training steps, but that wasn't good enough for the *procuratore generale* who complained to the Turin Court of Appeals. The court ruled that it was illegal for women to be lawyers and the decision was upheld by the Supreme Court of Cassation.

A majority of newspapers supported women in public roles. The American Minister to Italy was no help when he voiced his opinion that women did not belong in professions.

Poët, although limited in what she could do, worked in her brother's office. It wasn't until 1919 that she was allowed to join the Council of Lawyers.

She was active in the international woman's movement.

166. Clary Campoamor Rodriguez
Born 12 February 1888 Madrid, Spain
Died 30 April 1972 Lausanne, Switzerland

Feminist
Journalist
Lawyer
Politician
Seamstress
Teacher
Translator
Writer

Rodriguez probably holds some record for working in many professions.

She needed to study part time to pay for law school. Throughout her life at different times, she worked as: a journalist, lawyer, politician, seamstress, typing teacher and writer.

She was only the second woman to belong to the Madrid Bar

Association and the first to argue before the Spanish High Court. She represented Spain at the League of Nations.

When she worked as a journalist, she came in contact with feminist leaders. She is considered the mother of the Spanish feminist movement.

Her law practice dealt with family issues.

Although she couldn't vote, she won a place in Constituent Assembly where she fought hard for women's right to vote, arguing that excluding women was against natural law.

She lived in exile during the Spanish Civil War in Brazil and Switzerland, where she died.

167. Mary Ann Camberton Shadd Cary
Born 9 October 1823 Wilmington, Delaware
Died 5 June 1893 Washington, D.C. of stomach cancer

American Canadian Anti-Slavery Activist
Journalist
Lawyer
Publisher
Teacher

Shad could appear in several categories.

She was the first black woman publisher in North America and the first woman publisher in Canada and the second black woman to attend law school in the U.S.

The Provincial Freeman, which she edited, was established in 1853. Published weekly in southern Ontario, it advocated equality, integration and self-education for black people in Canada and the United States.

Shad's family was involved in the Underground Railroad, assisting those fleeing slavery. After the passage of the Fugitive Slave Act of

1850, her family relocated to Canada. She returned to the United States during the American Civil War where she recruited soldiers for the Union. Self-taught, she went to Howard University Law School, and continued advocacy for civil rights for African Americans and women for the rest of her life.

168. Margaret Bush Wilson
Born 30 January 1919 St. Louis, Missouri
Died 11 August 2009 St. Louis, Missouri

Activist
Lawyer

Wilson introduced President Ronald Reagan at a national NAACP conference by saying he revived "war, pestilence, famine, and death."

She was the second African American woman to pass the Missouri bar and be licensed.

As first woman on the NAACP board, she served nine terms but was relieved of many of the responsibilities after she suspended the executive director, finding him incompetent based on membership loss and financial problems.

She returned to her native St. Louis where she'd had been president of two NAACP chapters.

Her protests helped force businesses to hire blacks in jobs that only had hired whites.

Wilson lost an election for Congress.

She served as counsel for a case before the Supreme Court, Shelley v. Kraemer. A black family had been forced from their home by the Missouri Supreme Court based on a racial covenant. Missouri said the covenant was enforceable. The Supreme Court said it wasn't.

LIBRARIAN

To some, the image of a librarian is a spinsterish woman. To others she's a heroine who introduced them to a bigger world. Libraries vary from a van traveling the countryside to bring books to people who would not otherwise be able to get them to one with millions of volumes like the Bodleian at Oxford University. Four out of five librarians in the United States are women. From the Department of Professional Employees AFL/CIO for 2016:

- There were 17,000 U.S. public libraries
- Libraries circulated 2.23 billion print and electronic materials
- They offered 5.19 million programs, attended by 113 million members of the public.
- Children's programs accounted for 55% of all programs and served 77 million children and parents.

169. Pura Teresa Belpré y Nogueras
Born 2 February 1899 Cidra, Puerto Rico
Died 1 July 1982 New York, New York

Educator
Librarian
Writer

When Nogueras went to her sister's wedding in New York from Puerto Rico, she was offered and accepted a job offer with the New York Public Library (NYPI.) The library wanted a diversified staff.

It became her life's work.

She was the first Puerto Rican to work for NYPL. When she was transferred to the NYPL 115th Street branch, she advocated for the Spanish-speaking population and started Spanish language programs.

The library played host to Mexican artist Diego Rivera.

She began writing. A love story between a cockroach and a mouse was published.

During her marriage to Clarence Cameron White, a composer and violinist, she quit the library to write full-time. After his death and her retirement, she returned to the library parttime.

Her involvement in the South Bronx Library Project brought library services to the Latino community.

She continued to write and published *Juan Bobo and the Queen's Necklace: A Puerto Rican Folk Tale* in 1962.

LINGUIST/TRANSLATOR

As specialists in languages not just in speaking but understanding the intricacies, linguists' abilities can add to the knowledge of other disciplines. Without them translating and communication between cultures would be impossible.

Translators work more with the written word while an interpreter works with the verbal. They can be one with the goal of making sure speakers of different languages understand the same message. The American Translators Association's newsletter is read by 10,000 people in 100 countries. They offer certification of qualification. Shu Ni Lim reported the global language services market is valued at $60.68 billion. Europe has 49% of the market with North America having 39.41%. There are some 640,000 translators worldwide. There are places where translating and interpretation are considered more of a feminine position.

170. Lilias Eveline Armstrong
Born 29 September 1882 Pendlebury, England
Died 9 December 1937 North Finchley, England of a stroke

Editor
Educator
Linguist

Being multi-lingual is an accomplishment, but Armstrong went beyond the basics of vocabulary, speaking, writing and understanding a new language. She worked with the intonation and phonetics of languages including the African languages of Somali and Kikuyu as well as several European languages.

She taught in elementary school before moving to the University College Phonetics Department. There she taught the phonetics of French, English, French Swedish and Russian. She taught regular classes and in the vacation school.

Her books and papers include included:

- *A Handbook of English Intonation*, co-authored with Ida Ward
- *The Phonetic and Tonal Structure of Kikuyu*
- *The Phonetic Structure of Somali*
- *A Burmese Phonetic Reader with English Translation*
- *The Phonetics of French: A Practical Handbook*

She developed "ear tests" to help students learning a language hear the differences in the phonetics of the new language.

She became the subeditor of the International Phonetic Association's journal *Le Maître Phonétique.*

171. Kató Lomb
Born 8 February 1909 Pèces, Hungary
Died 9 June 2003 Budapest, Hungary

Interpreter
Linguist
Translator
Writer

Lomb had a unique way to learn languages. She knew 17 but could only interpret fluently in ten. Her favorite method of learning was to find an interesting novel in an unknown language. She didn't worry about what she missed on her first reading because she would figure it out.

She was one of the first simultaneous translators.

Her original studies were in physics and chemistry.

She was mostly self-taught and could work in Bulgarian, Chinese, Danish, English, French, German, Hebrew, Italian, Japanese, Latin, Polish, Romanian, Russian, Slovak, Spanish, Ukrainian. Her ability was to speak, read, write and translate.

According to her, she wanted more than the command of the language, but the study of them.

She considers Hungarian her mother tongue and her greatest fluencies are in English, German, French, and Russian.

In her book, *An Interpreter Around the World,* she wrote about her travels in 40 countries.

MAIL CARRIER

The first female postmaster, Mary Katherine Goddard from Baltimore, Maryland, was appointed in 1775 shortly after the United States Postal Service was founded. Sarah Black of Charleston, MD was the first female carrier in 1845. In 2024, 46% of the United States Postal Service employees are female.

172. Mary Fields (Stagecoach Mary and Black Mary)
Born c. 1832 Hickman County, Tennessee
Died 5 December 1914 Great Falls, Montana

Chambermaid
Laundry Owner
Mail Carrier
Servant
Tavern Owner

In the late 1800s postal deliveries in cities might have been easy, but much of America was country, plains, desert or forest routes.

Fields, a former slave, was the first black woman to be a Star Route postwoman. Her route was from Cascade, Montana to Saint Peter's Mission.

Prior to that role, she had many jobs.

After her emancipation, she worked as a chambermaid on a Mississippi River steamboat.

When she worked for a family where the wife died, she accompanied the widower's children to a convent and finally ended up in Montana.

She was a Jill-of-all-trades in the convent from tending chickens to making repairs, but the sisters barred her from the convent for her profane behavior. She then opened a tavern that went bankrupt from giving away too much free food to the poor.

She was 60 when she went to work for the U.S. Postal Service. She carried guns for protection and traveled by stagecoach. Sometimes she needed snowshoes for her deliveries.

MARTIAL ARTS

Martial arts are rule-based combat following traditions and strict rules. The different formats are used for combat, competitions, entertainment, law enforcement and military. Many can be tied to a nation's cultural heritage. Women faced cultural barriers and perceptions of women as being too weak to participate.

173. Keiko Fukuda
Born 12 April 1913 Tokyo, Japan
Died 9 February 2013 San Francisco, California

Educator
Martial Arts

Fukuda may have learned all the traditional Japanese arts that women were taught such as calligraphy, flower arranging and the tea ceremony, but it was judo that she cared most about.

Holding the judoka rank of 9th dan Kudokan in 2006, she was 10th dan USA Judo in 2011.

Inspired when she saw a judo training session, she pioneered women's judo.

She was only one of 35 women training at Kodokan. She studied under three masters. Two years later, this tiny woman at four foot eleven (150 cm) was teaching. She taught at Mills college in California for 11 years and become an American.

She wrote *Born for the Mat: A Kodokan Kata Textbook for Women* and later *Ju-No-Kata*.

She also taught in Australia, Canada, France and Norway, continuing to do three classes a week until she died.

MATHEMATICIANS

Mathematics is and never has been considered an area that women excel in. Some women were able to break through the prejudice to do the work. Having it recognized was a second barrier.

174. Marie-Sophie Germain
Born 1 April 1776 Paris, France
Died 27 June 1831 Paris, France of breast cancer

Mathematician
Philosopher

Despite brilliant work in mathematics, when Germain died, her death certificate did not list her as a mathematician. Denial through her life between what she wanted to do and what she could accomplish did not stop her from trying and she often accomplished things other women might not have.

Her father, a silk merchant, had discouraged her education, although she had access to his library, where she spent much time after the Bastille fell because it was much safer indoors. Her family kept her bedroom cold to keep her from studying.

The *École Polytechnique* denied her admission.

Although denied a career because of her gender, she worked on complicated mathematic problems on her own including: Fermat's Last Theorem, elasticity theory, mean curvature, and the Sophie Germain Theorem.

Her work did receive some recognition: she was the first woman to win a prize from the *Académie des Sciences.*

Besides mathematics, she classified facts for psychology and sociology systems.

175. Elizabeth Lucar
Born 1510 London, England
Died 29 October 1537 London, England

Algorist
Calligrapher
Mathematician
Musician
Needleworker

Much of her work is clouded by time. She is known mostly by a poem on her tomb that was commissioned by her husband to immortalize her skills when she died at age 27. We know from that poem that she was fluent in Italian, Latin and Spanish, she had mathematical ability, and she could play the flute.

She was said to have written a book, *Beautiful and Curious Calligraphy,* allegedly published in 1525, probably the first book on the subject. No copies exist today.

Coming from a family of tailors and marrying a tailor, she used her mathematical skills for algorithms used in tailoring, a comment on her mathematical ability. *Algorisme* was considered as the mathematical basis of many crafts long before it was associated with computers.

She was the mother of five children.

176. Amalie Emmy Noether

Born 23 March 1882 Erkangen, Bavaria, Germany
Died 14 April 1935 Bryn Mawr, Pennsylvania after surgery for a
tumor

Mathematician

Noether's mind wasn't hampered by her gender, but her career was littered with roadblocks. Described by a brilliant mathematician as the most important woman in the history of mathematics, she wasn't paid for seven years by the Mathematical Institute of Erlangen.

She had similar problems at Göttingen University, being allowed to teach but without pay.

At Göttingen her hiring had been protested. One professor said, "What will our soldiers think when they return to the university and find that they are required to learn at the feet of a woman?"

While at Göttingen, she had a major influence on those that she worked with.

A paper she wrote was presented by a man.

When the Nazi government dismissed all Jews, she found a post at Bryn Mawr College. She also worked with the Institute for Advanced Study in Princeton, New Jersey.

Throughout her career, she made discoveries recognized by other mathematicians. Despite how she had been treated, she promoted the work of her students and others.

177. Mary Somerville

Born 26 December 1780 Jedburgh, Scotland
Died 29 November 1872 Naples, Italy

Astronomer
Businesswoman
Mathematician
Philosopher
Scientist
Writer

Her family had a limited income. Her mother supplemented the family income by growing vegetables. Her father insisted that his daughter be educated and enrolled her in a boarding school.

She was a natural scholar. She was intrigued by shells and other sea life which she found on the beach. She loved her father's library, but an aunt voiced the opinion she should not be allowed to waste time reading. An uncle, impressed by her self-taught Latin, took her under his educational wing. She fell into the study of algebra and geometry by discovering more books.

She studied mathematics and astronomy. Together with Caroline Herschel they were elected as the first women honorary members of the Royal Astronomical Society. Although well known in her time, her accomplishments have been dissipated by time.

When John Stuart Mill petitioned parliament to approve women having the right to vote, he made sure her signature was the first on the petition.

When she died the *Morning Post* called her the "queen of science."

MEDICAL DOCTORS

The medical field was especially hard for women to crack throughout the centuries. Some entered by back doors by becoming midwives. Others fought for opportunities to study. In 2022, U.S. women were dominate with over 50% of the practitioners in three areas: pediatrics, ob/gyn, diabetes/endocrinology. In other areas they represented 30% or more.

178. Safiye Ali
Born 2 February 1894 Istanbul, Turkey
Died 5 July 1952 Dortmund, Germany of cancer

Medical Doctor

It is a far cry from treating soldiers on the battlefield to concentrate on mother and child welfare.

Ali managed to do both.

She was the second woman doctor in Turkey having attended schools in Turkey and Germany before opening her own office in Istanbul in 1923.

Despite her credentials, she had problems. Wealthy patients preferred male doctors. Poor ones had problems paying.

Prejudice followed her when she was the first female lecturer to teach gynecology and obstetrics lessons at the American College to women. It was the first girls' medical school. When she resigned from Süt Damlası because of unfair treatment, it caused protests at the house of her replacement.

An early advocate of breast feeding, she considered diet important to health.

She opened the Hilal-i Ahmer Ladies Center Little Children Practice.

Politically, she belonged to the Women's People Party which worked under the name Women's Union.

To fight prostitution, she helped open a woman's shelter.

179. Kate Waller Barrett
Born 24 January 1857 Falmouth, Virginia
Died 23 February 1925 Stafford, Virginia

Medical Doctor
Social Reformer

Dr. Barrett, born into a slave-holding family, founded homes in 1885 to help the women whom society rejected.

Her sense of social reform was formed after observing social problems while traveling with her husband, Robert South Barrett, an Episcopal Minister. It was confirmed when a single mother and her child arrived at their door whose story was the start of Barrett's life's work.

Her husband encouraged her to pursue a medical degree. She did while raising six children.

When the family moved to London because of her husband's health, she studied at the Nightingale Training School.

She was widowed at age 39.

Her first rescue home for unwed mothers was in Atlanta, Georgia. It met with governmental opposition. The wealthy Charles Nelson Crittenton had been engaged in the same work.

They joined forces to create the National Florence Crittenton Mission. Crittenton was president, Barrett vice president.

When Crittenton died, Barrett became president. By the time of her death, over 70 homes existed.

180. Tewhida Ben Sheikh
Born 2 January 1909 Tunis, Tunesia
Died 6 December 2010

Doctor

When Ben Sheik finished her degree at the *Faculté de médecine de Paris* and returned home to Tunisia, the local doctors feted her at a dinner. She was the first Tunisian woman to become a medical doctor.

It had been hard. Her conservative mother had to be convinced by her teachers to let her study medicine.

Her specialty, gynecology, made her a pioneer in family planning, contraceptives and abortion at the women's clinic which she directed.

As the Tunisian Red Crescent vice president, she promoted the creation of several organizations that helped orphans, providing childcare and education.

Because she worked in highly populated areas with poor populations, she became known as "the doctor of the poor." Her services were often free.

181. Elizabeth Blackwell
Born 3 February 1821 Bristol, England
Died 31 May 1910 Hastings, England after a fall

Medical Doctor

Blackwell's belief that empathy was part of being a doctor was considered feminine by male doctors. Perhaps her beliefs came from her family who were pro-women. Rather than beat her children, her mother recorded bad behavior in a black book and when there were too many entries, she banished the child to the attic in an early version of "timeout."

Blackwell received the first U.S. medical degree and was the first woman registered on the General Medical Council in England. Blackwell's sister Emily was the second woman to get a U.S. medical degree.

Her applications to medical schools were rejected until Geneva Medical College said yes because male students, asked to vote on her admittance as a joke, said yes.

She studied midwifery in Europe but was not allowed other medical training.

As founder of the New York Infirmary for Women and Children she promoted girls' education.

182. Rebecca Lee Crumpler
Born 8 February 1831 Delaware, Maryland
Died 9 March 1895 Fairview, Massachusetts of fibroid tumors

Doctor
Nurse
Author

During the early 1860s in the U.S., out of 54,543 medical doctors, there were 300 women and one African American, Ruth Lee Crumpler. Her degree was from the New England Female Medical College where she was the only black student. Crumbler had previously been a nurse.

Her interest in medicine was influenced by her aunt who cared for the sick.

She wrote a book, *A Book of Medical Discourses,* from notes she had written during her practice.

In Boston she worked with the Freedman's Bureau, which assisted former slaves. Most of her patients were poor African American women and children.

Crumpler met with prejudice. One example of her being mocked was people saying M.D. stood for Mule Driver. Many pharmacies would not fill her prescriptions.

She and her second husband, a former slave, were buried in unmarked graves until 2020 when gravestones were placed in Fairview Cemetery.

183. Marie Josefina Durocher
Born 6 January 1809 Paris, France
Died 25 December 1893 Brazil

Midwife
Obstetrician

Duroche made a better doctor than dressmaker. After moving to Brazil from Paris at age eight, she worked in her mother's fashion shop.

After marrying and having two children, almost back-to-back, her mother died, her husband was murdered, and she lost the shop. Needing to earn a living, she started a midwife course but changed to the Medical School of Rio de Janeiro when it opened and was the first to earn a medical degree in Brazil in 1834.

Her approach was far from traditional. Not only did she dress in men's clothes, but changed the ways women's health was handled including dealing with rape and abortions. She crusaded for her improved techniques during her sixty-year career.

She was the first and only woman to be a female member of the *Academia Nacional de Medicina* in 1871. Her reputation was such that she was the midwife to the grandchildren of Emperor Pedro II of Brazil.

184. Marie Equi
Born 7 April 1872 New Bedford, Massachusetts
Died 13 July 1952 Portland, Oregon

Doctor
Feminist
Lesbian
Political Activist
Prisoner

Dr. Equi, the daughter of Irish and Italian immigrants, was ahead of her time. She was one of the first 60 women to earn a medical degree in Oregon.

She battled for women's health care, workers' rights, the vote and against war.

Although it was illegal, she provided birth control and abortions.

Wealthy women paid more.

As a lesbian, she adopted a child, an early example of same-sex adoption.

The United States Army commended her for her medical help during the 1906 San Francisco earthquake.

She supported workers at Canary Wharf, many who were women earning between five to eight cents per hour. When she saw a pregnant woman dragged off, her actions caused the police to club her.

She marched in anti-war protests carrying a banner "Prepare to Die Workingmen." Under the Espionage Act she was sentenced to three years in prison. President Woodrow Wilson commuted it to a year and a day.

In 1930, after a heart attack, she sold her medical practice.

185. Kate Campbell Hurd-Mead

Born 6 April 1867 Danville, Quebec
Died 1 January 1941 Haddam, Connecticut in a bush fire

Feminist
Obstetrician

Post-op lunches were just one way Dr. Hurd-Mead worked to improve women's roles in medicine and review procedures and results.

She was an avid promoter of the maternal hygiene and infant welfare models, and a devoted supporter of women physicians.

Her father had been a doctor. She received her M.D. in 1888 in Boston and did further study in Europe before moving to Baltimore, Maryland to become medical director of Bryn Mawr School. There she started a health program with physical exercise.

She co-founded the Evening Dispensary for Working Women and Girls in Baltimore, the first medical institution to employ women physicians in the city.

After she married, she moved to Middletown, Connecticut, and established a private practice plus nurses training programs.

She incorporated Middlesex County Hospital.

Her book, *History of Women in Medicine: From the Earliest of Times to the Beginning of the Nineteenth Century* in 1938 documented how her gender had worked in the profession.

186. Aletta Henriëtte Jacobs
Born 9 February 1854 Sappemeer, Netherlands
Died 10 August 1929 Baarn, Netherlands

Doctor
Suffragette

Pregnancy, some doctors said, is punishment for sin and giving women diaphragms circumvents the divine plan. Dr. Jacobs didn't care. She had already gone through hoops to become a doctor, the first in The Netherlands.

After only weeks in a finishing school that she termed "idiotic" she quit. She continued her studies at home before working in a pharmacy.

She appealed to a government minister to be allowed to attend medical school, the first woman to do so.

After graduation, she opened a clinic in Amsterdam to help working women with hygiene, prostitution and venereal diseases. She also tackled other issues including workplace conditions.

She fought for women's rights worldwide and was a moving light behind the Women's International League for Peace and Freedom.

She appealed a decision when told that women were not citizens and couldn't vote because husbands paid the taxes. The appeal that she paid taxes failed. The 1887 Constitution made sure only men could vote.

187. Sophiea Louisa Jex-Blake
Born 21 January 1840 Hastings, England
Died 7 January 1912 Mark Cross, England

Educator
Feminist
Medical Doctor

Finding acceptance at a medical school was a major challenge for Jex-Blake.

Despite parental objections, she attended Queen's College.

When she taught mathematics, her father would not let her accept a salary.

Harvard refused her admission in 1867.

Edinburgh University refused her.

Rather than accept rejection, Jex-Blake advertised for women to join her in seeking admission. They formed the Edinburgh Seven and were admitted to Edinburgh University in 1869, the first British university to allow women.

Opposition continued. A mob in what was called The Surgeons' Hall Riot threw mud at the women on 18 November 1870. Bowing to pressure, the university refused them degrees. The court sided with the university.

Women were finally admitted to degree programs in Scotland and other countries.

Dr. Jex-Blake opened an office in Edinburgh, catering to poor women. The first hospital was staffed entirely by women.

188. Mary Jane Safford-Blake
Born 31 December 1834 Hye Park, Vermont
Died 8 December 1891Tarpon Springs, Florida

Educator
Gynecologist
Suffragist

Safford-Blake's nickname was "Cairo Angel" for her nursing of soldiers during the Civil War. She accompanied the army of Ulysses S. Grant.

Exhausted from what she saw, she spent months in France and Italy. Once renewed she went to the New York Medical College and Hospital for Women in 1869. She did further studies at Vienna General Hospital, Breslau University and Heidelberg University.

Moving to Boston she had the title of Professor of Women's Diseases at Boston University School of Medicine. She also treated poor women, mostly immigrants in sections of Boston.

She lectured and wrote papers on issues such as the problems of women's clothing and the importance of pre-natal care.

Politically she believed in women's right to vote and served on the Boston School Committee.

Ill health forced an early retirement.

189. Clara Emilia Smitt-Dryselius
Born 4 January 1864 Stockholm, Sweden
Died 13 January 1928 Stockholm, Sweden

Hydro Therapist
Medical Doctor
Writer

Smitt was a foster child who would succeed first as a nurse then as a doctor promoting revolutionary ideas about light and water therapies in various sanatoriums, some started and managed by her and her husband Erland Dryselius. After her marriage, she hyphenated her name.

In 1892 she opened Saltsjöbadens, a sanatorium in a villa where she worked until 1902.

During the Greco-Turkish Wars she acted as a nurse and later received a Red Cross medal for her work.

Her interest in modern health methods grew out of her medical studies in Europe, especially those of hydro and light therapies. She returned to Sweden and promoted the idea that healthy living in the form of good diets and exercise contributed to good health as well as regular medicines.

Her publications also dealt with women's rights.

MIDWIVES

In 2021 only 12% of U.S. births were attended by midwives. Many insurance companies still will not cover their costs. The American College of Nurse-Midwives (ACNM) is the Professional association representing certified nurse-midwives (CNMs) in the United States.

190. Marie-Anne Victoire Gillain Boivin
Born 9 April 1773 Versailles, France
Died 16 May 1841

French Midwife
Inventor

Boivin may have written an obstetrics book, *Memorial de l'Art des Accouchemens*, that included 41 plates and 116 self-hand-colored figures, but she was never accepted into the French Academy of Medicine. The book would be used for 150 years. She was able, however, to join other medical societies.

She invented a pelvimeter, a vaginal speculum, and was a pioneer in using a stethoscope to listen to fetal heartbeats. She discovered reasons for some cases of bleeding, miscarriages, placenta and uterus problems that were not previously known. She was the first to remove a cancerous cervix.

Because of her work on spontaneous abortion, the Royal Society of Medicine at Bordeaux gave her a commendation.

Despite her accomplishments, she did have problems. Jealous

colleagues forced her resignation, and she worked at a hospital for fallen women at low wages, dying in poverty.

191. Angélique Marguerite Le Boursier du Coudray
Born c. 1712 Clermont-Ferrand, France
Died 17 April 1794 Bordeaux, France

Midwife

As a midwife, she changed the emphasis of care of the mother and ignoring a dying infant. She tried to work on both.

At the time she became a midwife, men were taking over the field. She was lucky enough to be certified at the *École de Chirurgie* three years before women were barred, although she fought the decision, saying it could limit the number of well-trained midwives.

In 1759, she published an early midwifery textbook, *Abrégé de l'Art des Accouchements,* an update of a 1667 text.

By traveling throughout France, she was able to train 4,000 students who passed their knowledge to others. Her course, leading to certification, lasted six weeks of all-day classes. Although there was a cost, not every woman passed. It covered anatomy, prenatal care and handling both normal and problem births.

Her invention of a mannequin, a realistic representation of a woman in labor, helped in training.

192. Mary Carson Breckinridge
Born 17 February 1881 Memphis, Tennessee
Died 16 May 1965 Hyden, Kentucky

Midwife
Nurse

The Frontier Nursing Service (FNS), started by Breckinridge, treated 58,000 patients and delivered 14,500 babies, with only 11 maternal deaths between 1939 and 1965. Many nurses reached their patients by horseback.

Breckenridge was born into a political family boasting of high governmental officials. While the boys in her family were educated in private schools, she had private tutors and governesses as the family moved between states and countries.

She became a registered nurse in 1910. She worked in Washington D.C. slums and supervised nurses through the 1918 flu epidemic.

Realizing the need for trained midwives in rural areas, especially Kentucky, she did research by traveling through the area on horseback which supplemented her earlier extensive research.

As a volunteer in France after World War I, she helped restore supply chains. At this point she concentrated on small children, pregnant women and new mothers.

She was also a white supremacist.

193. Marie-Louise Lachapelle
Born 1 January 1769 Paris, France
Died 4 October 1821 Paris, France of stomach cancer

Midwife
Writer

Lachapelle was the daughter and granddaughter of midwives. Her father was a health official. Considered the mother of modern obstetrics, she was taught midwifery by her mother from the age of 12.

Her first delivery had complications, but mother and baby survived.

She published textbooks about women's bodies, gynecology, and obstetrics. promoting natural deliveries.

Although she stopped working when she married, after her husband's death she returned to midwifery to support her daughter.

In 1797, when her mother died, Lachapelle took over her mother's role as head of Hôtel-Dieu, the top obstetric hospital in Paris.

The minister of the interior invited her to direct a midwifery school.

Lachapelle went to Heidelberg for more study.

Unfortunately, she died before finishing *The Practice of Deliveries: or Chosen Observations and Memories on the Most Important Points of the Art*. It was completed by her nephew and was used for most of the 19th century.

MILITARY

The simple definition of soldier is anyone who serves in the military.

Joan of Arc and Boudica notwithstanding, women in the military were always a minority but have served in various capacities since the beginning of time. Patriotic women often fought for their countries or beliefs well before they were officially allowed to do so.

Many countries have had women who have had outstanding careers in their military. Sometimes, women dressed as men so they could serve.

As of 2020 the U.S. Army had 16,987 women officers and 57,605 enlisted females. President Truman signed the Women's Armed Services Integration Act in June 1948, allowing women to serve in all branches of the military.

In 2021 in the United States, women made up 17.3% of the active-duty force of 231,741 members; and 21.4% of the National Guard and reserves at 171,000 members.

194. Lilian Bader
Born 18 February 1918
Died 13 March 2015

Soldier
Teacher

Orphaned at age nine, Bader was placed in a convent until she was 20.

Attempts to find work were unsuccessful because she was half West Indian. As she said, "… not even the priests dare risk ridicule by employing me."

She was the first black woman to join the British armed forces, Navy, Army and Air Force Institutes (NAAFI).

Prejudice continued. She only served seven weeks because they discovered her father was from Barbados. He had been a merchant seaman in World War I.

The Royal Air Force accepted her mixed heritage and she was one of the first women trained in instrument repair.

She married a tank driver and was discharged when she became pregnant.

After the war, she went to London University and became a teacher.

195. Pancha Carrasco
Born 8 April 1816 Cartago, Costa Rica
Died 31 December 1890 San Jose, Costa Rica

Cook
Medic
Soldier

With a rifle and a handful of bullets Carrasco joined the fighters at the 1856 Battle of Rivas, making her the first known Costa Rican woman to do military service. Her duties also included serving as a cook and medic. Those chores did not slow her use of her rifle.

She was of mixed heritage: American, African and European.

From the beginning, she did not follow society's rules of her time. She insisted on learning to read and write. She became an excellent rider.

She fought against William Walker, an American doctor, lawyer, journalist and mercenary. A believer in the U.S. manifest destiny, he organized military expeditions to Costa Rica and other Latin American countries with the goal of creating slave-holding colonies.

When she was working as a cook, she was said to keep her apron full of bullets.

196. Susan Ahn Cuddy

Born 16 January 1915 Los Angeles, California
Died 24 June 2015 Los Angeles, California

Gunnery Officer

A trail blazer in several ways, Cuddy was like her parents who were the first married Korean immigrant couple in California. Her parents' on-going fight to free Korea from Japanese control influenced her to join Korean independence groups.

She failed in her attempt to join the Women Accepted for Voluntary Emergency Service after Pearl Harbor but was accepted at the U.S. Naval Reserve Midshipmen's School, making her the first Asian-American woman in the Navy. The prevailing viewpoint was women did not belong in military service.

Her first assignment was as an instructor teaching men.

Her trail-blazing credentials continued when she became the first female aerial gunnery officer.

At different times, she worked for the U.S. Navy Intelligence, Library of Congress and the National Security Agency. At one point she headed a 300-person think tank.

She disobeyed anti-miscegenation laws and her mother's disapproval when she married an Irish American.

She remained politically active throughout her life and died at age 100.

197. Florence Beatrice Green
Born 19 February 1901 Edmonton, England
Died 4 February 2012 North Lynn, England

Veteran

Green had Women's Royal Air Force service number 22,360 and was one of the last surviving members of World War I. She joined the service at age 17 and was stationed at RAF Marham and Narborough airfield where she served food and beverages, freeing up a man for other duties.

After the war she had three children with her husband Walter Green, also a veteran. Their 55- year marriage ended with his death.

On her 110th birthday she was asked how it felt to be 110 and she replied, "Not much different from being 109." Her children said that their mother didn't talk about her service, which remained undiscovered until 2008 when research by a gerontology researcher revealed her information.

She died in her sleep.

198. Mary Agnes Halleran
Born 4 May 1907 Lowell, Massachusetts
Died 13 February 2005 McLean, Virginia

Educator
Soldier

Being barely five feet did not stop Hallaren from becoming the third director of the Women's Army Corps (WAC). When being recruited and asked about her size, she said, "You don't have to be six feet tall to have a brain that works."

She was made Captain in 1943 and commanded the first women's battalion to go overseas.

Before World War II, she taught junior high school.

By 1945, she was in command of WAC personnel in Europe and had earned the rank of Lieutenant Colonel.

She worked with Generals Dwight D. Eisenhower and George C. Marshall to merge the women's corps with the regular Army. Her serial number was L-1 when she became the first woman to serve as an officer in the Regular Army.

She retired at 53 and was considered part of *The Greatest Generation* by Tom Brokaw.

199. Joy Bright Hancock
Born 4 May 1898 Wildwood, New Jersey
Died 20 August 1986 Bethesda, Maryland

Editor
Pilot
U.S. Naval Officer
Hancock was a veteran of both World Wars.

She enlisted in the Navy after finishing business school. Later education included degrees from George Washington University, the Crawford School of Foreign Service, the Pierce School of Business Administration in Philadelphia, and the Paris Branch of the New York School of Fine Arts.

Her first and second husbands were killed in airship crashes.

Working at the Bureau of Aeronautics, she edited a newsletter and later *Naval Aviation News*. After attending the Foreign Service School, she handled their public affairs activities.

She received her pilot's license.

When the Women Accepted for Volunteer Emergency Service (WAVES) was formed she joined and was commissioned a

Lieutenant. Later she was promoted to Lieutenant Commander and finally Commander.

She worked on the integration of women into the Naval Service.

After the war she became the Assistant Director (Plans) of the Women's Reserve and then the WAVES' Director and finally Captain. Her promotions were one of the fastest tracks in U.S. Navy history.

200. Sheila Anne Hellstrom
Born 15 January 1935 Lunenburg, Nova Scotia
Died 7 December 2020 Ontario, Canada

Brigadier General

Hellstrom was the first woman to graduate from the Canadian Forces College and the first to reach the rank of Brigadier General.

She told a magazine that her interest in the military came from stories told by Norwegian soldiers visiting her home during World War II. To fulfill that dream she enrolled in the Royal Canadian Air Force at the age of 19.

She worked her way through the ranks: flying officer, flight lieutenant, lieutenant colonel, and colonel in various postings including personnel administrations officer in several Canadian cities. She was the chair of the NATO Committee on Women.

Hellstrom worked for the recruitment and integration of women into the Canadian Forces.

She also earned a biology/chemistry degree from Mount Allison University.

After her retirement she worked with the military on gender and integration issues.

201. Kathleen Florence Lynn
Born 28 January 1874 Killala, County Mayo, Ireland
Died 14 September 1955 Baldsbridge, Ireland

Activist
Army Captain
Hospital Founder
Medical Doctor

At her funeral Dr. Lynn received full miliary honors while nurses lined the street, a perfect commentary of her life — military and medical.

At 16 she had decided to follow medicine.

Gender prejudice haunted her throughout her career.

Two appointments didn't work. When she was offered an appointment to an Adelaide hospital, it met with staff opposition. She did not take up the post.

She became the first female resident at Victoria Eye and Ear Hospital.

She founded St. Ultan's Hospital, run by women. It specialized in neo-natal care.

On the military side, she was the Medical Officer for the Irish Citizens Army in the 1916 Easter Rising.

It cost her family's support and led to imprisonment.

Being a Sinn Fein leader led to another arrest.

She was active in the Irish Women's Suffragette and Local Government Association, British Women's Social and Political Union.

During the 1918 flu pandemic she found homes for German children and worked in soup kitchens.

She was elected to the Dáil Éireann but didn't serve as part of the Sinn Féin abstentionist policy.

202. Roza Georgiyevna Shanina
Born 3 April 1924 Edma Velsky-Uyzed, Vologda Governorate, Russia
Killed in action 28 January 1945 Reichau, East Prussia, Russia

Kindergarten Worker
Sniper
Soldier

Shanina wanted to be on the frontline during World War II. She made 59 kills. Named after Marxist revolutionary Rosa Luxemburg, she was described as "the unseen terror of East Prussia."

Against her parents' wishes, she left home to study, where she joined the Soviet youth movement, Komsomol.

To help finance her education, she worked in a kindergarten. When the town where she was living was firebombed by the Germans, she did rooftop vigils to protect the kindergarteners.

Her brother's death motivated her to be a front-line sniper. In response to it, she learned shooting skills at the Central Women's Sniper Training School and her military training at the *Vsevobuch* program for universal military training. She refused to become an instructor, preferring to be on the front lines. She became a platoon commander.

Her first reaction to killing a man bothered her. In time, her opinion about taking the life of others changed.

A diary recorded her experiences.

Two soldiers found her body disemboweled.

203. María Josefa Gabriela Cariño de Silang

Born 19 March 1731 Santa, Ilocos Sur, Captaincy General of the
Philippines, Spanish Empire

Executed 20 September 1763 Capitaincy, Philippines (Spanish
Empire)

Military Leader

Sometimes compared to Joan of Arc, Silang became the female leader
of the independence movement from Spain.

As a child she was separated from her pagan mother. She was raised
and educated by a priest. He married her to a well-to-do businessman.
Three years later she was widowed. She then married Diego Silang
in 1757.

The Vigan area was in turmoil during the British and Spanish
Seven Years War. Manila fell to the British, but not Vigan. She and
her husband's goal was shown in the slogan, "wrest power from the
principales and restore it to the people."

They had some success.

Gabriela swore to avenge the assassination of her husband. Her
fighting force of 2,000 men lost.

She was captured and hung.

204. Mary Anne Talbot (John Taylor)
Born 2 February 1778 London, England
Died 4 February 1808

Sailor
Soldier

Talbot's life reads like a bad novel. Her claim that she was a baron's daughter is doubtful, but there were funds for her education and an inheritance.

Her lover, Captain Bown, enlisted her as a sailor on the Santo Domingo.

Her military career continued as a drummer boy for the 82nd Regiment of Foot at the battle of Valenciennes.

Talbot's troubles continued when she learned that her inheritance had been squandered.

She became a cabin boy on a French ship. When that ship was captured, she worked as a powder monkey, a job reserved for boys between 12-14 because they moved easily carrying ammunition.

When wounded in the leg, she was partially disabled.

She was imprisoned twice, once in a Dunkirk dungeon, once in Newgate Debtor Prison.

She quit as a clerk on an American ship because the skipper's niece was making advances, unaware of Talbot's gender.

She continued to dress as a man.

205. Ecaterina Teodoroiu
Born 15 January 1894 Vandeni, Romania
Died 3 September 1917 Muncelu, Romania from machine gun fire

Nurse
Soldier

Teodoroiu is another woman who has been compared to Joan of Arc. It seems the thing to do with a woman in the military.

She began as a civilian nurse in World War I and became a soldier after her brother died from war wounds.

When she was wounded in both legs, she spent almost three months in the hospital. After her release she asked to join her brother's 43/59 Infantry Regiment as a voluntary nurse.

On 17 March 1917 she received the honorary rank of Second Lieutenant from King Ferdinand and was given command of a 25-man platoon in the 7th Company (43/59 Infantry Regiment, 11th Division), becoming the first female Romanian Army officer.

Although asked to stay behind the lines, she refused. On 3 September 1917 as she was leading her platoon, a machine gunfire hit her in the chest. Her last words were said to be, "Forward, men, don't give up, I'm still with you!"

MOUNTAIN CLIMBER

In Wikipedia's long list of mountain climbers, almost all the names are men. Every now and then a woman's name pops up.

206. Wanda Rutkiewicz
Born 4 February 1943 Plungė, Lithuania
Died 12–13 May 1992 Kangchenjunga, Nepal. Her body was never found

Engineer
Mountain Climber

During her career, Rutkiewicz climbed ten mountains, although the tenth led to her death.

From a multi-sportive family, her passion was for mountain climbing. She was the first woman to reach the summit of K2 and the first European woman to summit Mount Everest. Her goal had been to climb the 14 major mountains.

Often frustrated by treatment of women climbers, she helped organize all-women expeditions.

Mexican mountaineer Carlos Carsolio said he had unsuccessfully tried to convince her not to make the climb on the day she disappeared. A body was found in a crevice at 7,700 meters in 1992 but was never identified as Rutkiewicz's.

Health issues, anemia in particular, caused her to take iron injections with her on climbs.

She graduated from Wroclaw University of Technology as an electrical engineer.

NURSES

Nursing has always been a woman's profession. Phoebe, mentioned in Romans 16:1. is one of the first nurses found in any document. Rufaidah bint Sa'ad was known as the first Muslim nurse in the seventh century. The modern concept of nursing began in the late nineteenth century in Germany and spread throughout the world, expanding from religious organizations and estates. Formal training was introduced and by the world wars nurses served a vital part of any army.

207. Sister Elizabeth Kenny
Born 20 September 1880 Warialda, New South Wales, Australia
Died 30 November 1952 Toowoomba, Queensland, Australia of Parkinson's Disease

Nurse
Music Teacher
Religious Teacher

Kenny, a self-trained bush nurse, treated some 7,800+ cases in her lifetime, working in Australia, Europe and the U.S.

When recovering from a broken disk at 17, she studied anatomy books where she learned about muscles. She made her own skeleton.

Never did she call herself a bush nurse. While working on transport ships, she described herself as *Nurse Kenny, Certificated Medical, Surgical, and Midwifery.*

She reached her patients by walking, riding a horse or buggy.

When she opened St. Canice to treat patients, she insisted strict regulations be followed.

She provided nursing services to World War I soldiers after paying her own way to Europe.

Since she was not a qualified nurse, she was sent to a transport not a hospital.

She helped a station owner's child recover from polio with her methods. She substituted hot compresses from plaster casts and physical therapy. Her method of treating polio was controversial.

208. Baroness Eva Charlotta Lovisa Sofia (Sophie) Mannerheim
Born 21 December 1863 Helsinki, Finland
Died 9 January 1928 Helsinki, Finland

Bank Employee
Nurse

Although a baroness and daughter of Count Carl Robert Mannerheim and sister of a former Finnish President, Carl Gustaf Emil Mannerheim, it was her work as a nurse in Finland that marked her contributions.

She first worked as a bank cashier until her 1896 marriage. That marriage failed.

In 1902 she attended the Nightingale School, St Thomas' Hospital in London.

When she began as head nurse of Helsinki Surgical Hospital, she found their methods were outdated. Her reforms met with opposition.

For 24 years she was President of the Finnish Nurses' Association and also was President of the International Council of Nurses.

Together with Arvo Yippö, she founded the Lastanlinna Children's Castle Hospital, incorporating international concepts. It mainly served single mothers. It is now part of Helsinki University Central

Hospital. Mannerheim is considered a pioneer in Finnish nursing methods.

209. Gladys Skillett
Born 2 May 1918 Guernsey, Channel Islands
Died 11 February 2010

Nurse
Prisoner

Women's friendships can survive the hatred of war.

Skillett, a nurse, was one of 834 people from the Baliwick of Guernsey during World War II to be deported to the Lindele internment camp near Biberach, Germany.

There she gave birth to a son, the first woman and Channel Islander to give birth in German captivity.

While in the hospital, she met Maria Koch, a German, who also had just given birth to a son.

Skillett's husband was also a prisoner at the camp. Koch's husband was in the Wehrmacht.

They began an unlikely friendship after they were released from the hospital by talking through the fence surrounding the camp. The friendship included Skillet providing supplies for Koch at the end when supplies were limited.

That friendship would continue after the camp was liberated in April 1945.

Sixty years after their birth, those two boy babies, David Skillett and Heiner Koch, participated together in Biberach's *Schützenfest*. One of Gladys's daughters marched with them.

PATHOLOGISTS

According to www.zippia.com 59.3% of American pathologists are women but earn 82% of what men do. African Americans make up 5.2% and Hispanics are 9.9%.

210. Sophia Getzowa
Born 10 January 1872 Belarus
Died 8 July 1946 Jerusalem, Israel

Pathologist
Scientist

Getzowa had her research taken by her director, Theodor Langhans, who used it for his Swiss living/working permission. He won a contested post as head of the Institute of Pathology over her. Getzowa became his first assistant.

During World War I, she substituted for him during his military duty. Two years later, she was dismissed.

Getzowa studied medicine at Bern University where she joined the Zionist movement. Although productive professionally, the breakup with her fiancé and the death of her sister left her grief stricken.

Her research morphed into lifelong interest in the thyroid. Throughout her career, she made major discoveries.

As a woman, a Jew and a foreigner, finding permanent work was difficult until she met Albert Einstein. His recommendation to a still-to-be-founded pathological institute resulted in an offer as director.

While waiting, she worked at Tel Aviv hospitals.

Getzowa was appointed lecturer at Jerusalem Hebrew University. They refused to recognize her as a professor. International colleagues helped her fight it. She was finally given professor emeritus status.

211. Alessandra Giliani
Born c 1307 Emilia-Romagna, Italy
Died 26 March 1326 possibly of a septic wound

Anatomist
Pathologist

Maybe she existed, maybe she didn't. Because women in this field at this time were so rare, she could have been removed from most historical documents. Another theory is that the Church burned any records about her.

It is said that she was a surgical assistant to a famous professor at the University of Bologna, Mondino de' Liuzzi, who wrote a major text. An illustrated manuscript has a drawing of de' Liuzzi with a young woman in the background giving credence to the story that Giliani existed and worked with him preparing cadavers for autopsy.

Giliani is said to have developed methods to drain blood from corpses which added to the understanding of the human circulatory system. To do her work, it is said, she disguised herself as a man.

PHOTOGRAPHERS

Hannah Rooke in a March 2022 article in *Digital Camera World* wrote, "Ask any female or female-identifying as a photographer, at one point or another she/they would've been talked down to, sexually harassed, belittled or made to feel uncomfortable by their male counterpart. Sadly, misogyny within the photography community is still rife." Despite that, many talented women photographers have been able to capture people and things reflecting humanity.

212. Imogen Cunningham
Born 12 April 1883 Portland, Oregon
Died 23 June 1976 San Francisco, California

Photographer

Cunningham combined the artistry of photography with chemistry research.

Her first camera bought at age 18 was from the American School of Art via mail order.

A few years later she started taking pictures seriously. Photographing plants for the botany department helped her pay for her Washington University chemistry degree. Her thesis was *Modern Processes of Photography.*

One of her projects at her first job was documenting American Indian tribes. Working with Edward S. Curtis they produced *The North American Indian.* He also taught her platinum printing techniques.

During a grant to study at the *Technische Hochschule*, she helped the chemistry department find less expensive printing methods and wrote *About the Direct Development of Platinum Paper for Brown Tones.*

In Seattle she opened her own studio and was known for her portraits, although a scandal arose with her nude photo of a male.

Her subjects varied over the years to include plants, industrial landscapes, hands of artists, street photography.

213. Vivian Dorothy Maier
Born 1 February 1926 New York, New York
Died 21 April 2009 Chicago, Illinois from injuries after a fall

Nanny
Street Photographer

For 40 years she worked as a nanny. The Gensburg family, for whom she worked, called her a real live Mary Poppins. How the family felt about her taking her charges on the photographing safaris to places like the stockyards is unknown. The Gensburgs helped her find an apartment when she was old and poor.

She had grown up in France and the U.S.

From 1959 to 1960 she photographed her way around the world with money from the sale of a French family farm.

Some of her photos were auctioned to pay for a storage bill. John Maloof bought about 30,000 negatives for research. Publishing them on his blog made them go viral.

Legal issues arose about ownership after family members were found in France. Cook County Illinois has set up an estate with proceeds of sales going between the estate and Maloof.

Maier only received recognition after her death for the 150,000+ photographs of people and architecture she took, thanks to the internet and Flickr.

214. Lucia Moholy (Lucy Shultz)
Born 18 January 1894 in Prague, Czech
Died 17 May 1989 Zurich, Switzerland

Photographer

Moholy had a lifelong struggle for recognition that often went to her husband László Moholy-Nagy and/or to Walter Gropius.

She learned her photographer skills at *Hochschule für Grafik und Buchkunst* in Leipzig.

Her photography supported her marriage to László Moholy-Nagy. The couple separated.

Walter Gropius, a German American architect and founder of the Bauhaus movement, had the plates of her photos documenting the Bauhaus architecture. He used them to help introduce and sell to a post-World War II audience. However, Moholy revoked their friendship after he failed to credit her.

Her personal life was unsettled and nomadic, abruptly leaving Berlin after a Communist MP, whom she was involved with, was arrested in her apartment.

She lived in a variety of countries, settling finally in the UK. An attempt for a U.S. visa failed.

She did find some success in commercial photography, teaching publishing and exhibiting.

215. Yevonde Philone Middleton
(Professional name Madame Yevonde)
Born 5 January 1893 London, England
Died 22 December 1975 London, England

Photographer
Suffragist

Middleton's heroine was Mary Wollstonecraft, so it is little wonder she was a suffragist, but she is mainly known for photography and is considered a pioneer in the use of color.

She was said to be independent from childhood, which matched her liberal education in England, France and Belgium. After school, she answered an ad for an apprentice photographer.

With financial backing from her father after her apprenticeship, she opened her own studio, building her reputation with free portraits that were published in society publications.

Her style was different from traditional portraits. For example, her subjects might look away from the camera or hold a prop. Her experiments with color photography, one of the first, were not always well accepted and she eventually returned to black and white.

However, she believed women were better suited to color photography because of their interest in color.

She worked up until her death at 83. Her photographs can be found on Google images.

POLITICANS

Women in United States politics have always been in the minority, although they are making inroads over the last few decades starting in 1917 with Janet Rankin from Montana. As of 2023, 29% of the delegates in the United States House of Representatives were women. In the 39th Canadian Parliament the figure was 21%. Between 1918 and 2024, 564 women have served in the United Kingdom's House of Commons. Women have served in top roles. In the United Kingdom they have had three women Prime Ministers. In the United States there has been one Vice President. Women candidates are now more likely to be seriously considered.

216. Georgina Beyer
Born November 1957 Wellington, New Zealand
Died 6 March 2023 Wellington, New Zealand of kidney problems

Activist
Drag Queen
Transgender Politician

She was the first transgender Labour Party member of the New Zealand Parliament and a tireless fighter for Mäori rights, LBGTQ rights, civil marriages, anti-discrimination laws and kinder prostitution laws. among other progressive issues.

Assigned as male at birth, her childhood was anything but stable with her mother divorcing and remarrying, giving another child up for adoption and leaving Georgina with her grandparents. She changed schools often, going from private to public.

At boarding school, she tried suicide.

- At 16 she left school to try for a career in acting.
- In 1979 she was violently sexually assaulted.
- In 1984 she had gender affirming surgery.

Back in Carleton, New Zealand, she won a place on the school board, then became mayor and was the first transgender person and first Māori. She resigned the post in 2000 when elected to Parliament. She was re-elected two years later but resigned in 2007.

217. Anita Lee Blair

Born 8 September 1916 Oklahoma City, Oklahoma
Died 2010 El Paso, Texas of a heart attack

Legislator

Losing her sight in a 1936 car crash did not stop Anita Lee Blair from living a full life. She was the first blind woman to serve in any state legislature.

After attending the Seeing Eye Dog School in Morristown, New Jersey she was given Fawn, a German Shepherd. The dog would later save her life in a hotel fire, leading Blair down multiple staircases to safety.

She earned a B.S. from Texas College of Mines and Metallurgy and an M.S. and an M.A. from Texas Woman's College.

An advocate of dog guide schools, she gave talks and advice. She would show a short movie, *A Day with Fawn*. For seven years she ran a lecture business without assistance.

Improved education was part of her legislative platform. She lost the first time, won the second.

During her term she won some of her issues but lost on a bill to allow women to serve on juries.

Fawn died in 1953. Blair continued to fight for her issues until her death in 2010.

218. Hattie Ophelia Watt Caraway
Born 1 February 1878 Bakerville, Tennessee
Died 21 December 1950 Falls Church, Virginia

Politician

"Silent Hattie" Caraway was appointed to the U.S. Senate when her husband died to fill his term, but in 1932 she won a full term as a Democrat.

She had been a housewife and mother before her first term. Her interest in politics had been limited. For the right to vote she said, "After equal suffrage I just added voting to cooking and sewing and other household duties."

She had the opportunity to preside over the Senate, the first woman to do so. She lost the primary in 1944 to William Fulbright.

She voted against the anti-lynching bill but co-sponsored the Equal Rights Amendment. Her stance for the G.I. Bill did not sit well with many congressmen who felt it was socialist. She agreed with the New Deal.

Although rare, her last day in the Senate was marked by a standing ovation.

219. Martha Wright Griffiths

Born 29 January 1912 Pierce City, Missouri
Died 22 April 2003 Amada, Missouri

Judge
Lawyer
Politician

Griffith's father thought that girls were smarter than boys, she said.

As a lawyer, judge and later a congresswoman, Griffiths pushed to include sex discrimination under Title VII of the Civil Rights Act of 1964.

From 1923 to 1970 the Equal Rights Amendment was stalled in a committee. Griffiths pushed to have it brought to the floor and won. It still did not pass.

She could be credited with many firsts. With experience as a lawyer and judge, she was the first woman to serve in the House, serving nine terms. She was the first woman to be a judge in the recorder's Court in Detroit.

Her husband, Hicks George Griffiths, was also a lawyer, a judge and was chairman of the Michigan Democratic Party. "I don't know really that I have so much perseverance as I do a sense of indignity at the fact that women are not justly treated. I have the same sort of feeling for Blacks, Latinos and the Asiatics."

After her stint in Congress, she became Lieutenant Governor of Michigan.

220. Alexandra Mikhailovna Kollontai
Born 9 March 1872 St. Petersburg, Russia
Died 1952 Moscow, Russia

Diplomat
Marxist Theoretician
Politician
Revolutionary

Kollontai was the first woman to become an official of a government cabinet when in 1917 she became part of Vladimir Lenin's government. Only one other woman, Maria Spiridonova, had such a prominent role.

She espoused radical politics from the later 19th century prior to joining with the Bolsheviks.

A rebellious child, she ran away from home to marry. She later left him and her children to work in politics.

When she was exiled from Russia in 1908, she visited Europe and the U.S. only returning to Russia after the 1917 Russian Revolution.

She became an important figure in promoting women's rights after seeing the horrible conditions of working women.

Throughout her career, she often was on the wrong side but bounced back to accept diplomatic roles in Norway, Mexico and Sweden, including an ambassadorship in Sweden.

There were times she feared for her life because of her positions.

221. Hazel McCallion
Born 14 February 1921 Port Daniel, Quebec, Canada
Died 29 January 2023 Mississauga, Canada of pancreatic cancer

Ice Hockey Player
Leader
Politician

McCallion was known as Hurricane Hazel and a Force of Nature. She was the longest serving mayor of Mississauga with 12 consecutive terms. Her political style was not to take political donations, instead asking her supporters to make donations to charity, not her.

Unable to afford college, she attended secretarial school then worked for an engineering company until she entered politics in 1967 where she sat on almost every committee possible until she was elected Mississauga Mayor.

She helped evacuate 200,000 residents after the 1979 Mississauga train derailment.

Not bad for an ex-professional ice hockey player.

Her chosen retirement was not relaxed. Among her many roles were:
- Greater Toronto Airport Authority board member
- Ontario government special advisor
- Sheridan College chancellor

She continued doing her own housework saying, "Housework and gardening are great forms of exercise and keep one humble."

She organized other mayors in the Greater Toronto area to work together on mutual concerns.

Dignitaries at her state funeral included two prime ministers and the Ontario Premier. Flags flew at half-mast.

222. Maureen O'Carroll
Born 29 March 1913 Galway, Ireland
Died 9 May 1984 Dublin, Ireland in her sleep

Civil Servant
Politician
Teacher

One of her accomplishments when she, as a member of the Irish Labour Party and a Teachta Dála (TD), was the removal of the word "illegitimate" from birth certificates.

One of her major influences had been her father, a participant in the Easter Uprising and a journalist.

She became a novice nun at Gortnor Abbey but decided that religious life was not the life she wanted. After leaving the Abbey she became a civil servant then a schoolteacher.

Her marriage to Gerard O'Carroll produced 11 children.

When she founded the Lower Prices Council, it was to fight high prices, scarcities and the black market. She sought higher office, losing in her first attempt, but succeeded and was elected to the Dublin North–Central constituency.

Her efforts helped introduce women to the Garda Síochána, the national police and security service.

223. Ana Pauker

Born 13 February 1893 Codăeşti, Vaslui County, Romania
Died 3 June 1960 Bucharest, Romania of cancer and heart failure

Politician
Translator

Pauker and her husband Marcel joined the Romanian Socialist Party
in 1918. For their controversial activities they exiled themselves to
Berlin, Paris and Vienna.

On her return to Romania, she was shot in both legs and sentenced
to ten years in prison until a prisoner exchange was made with the
Soviets in May 1941.

After the war and back in Romania, she became part of the
government as foreign minister, the first woman in a post of that
importance. She turned down other posts because she was a woman
but wielded power behind the scenes as a Stalinist and Moscow's
local agent.

She allegedly recruited 500,000 new Communist Party members.

Pauker promoted leniency in sentencing non-party members. She
often opposed the popular or Stalinist viewpoints such as allowing
peasants to have their own farms.

Born as an Orthodox Jew, she helped 100,000 Jews emigrate to
Israel.

Torture followed her arrest and was followed by house arrest.

Her last working years were as a translator.

224. Alice Mary Robertson
Born 2 January 1854 Tallahassee Mission, Muscogee Nation, Oklahoma
Died 1 July 1931 Muskogee, Oklahoma

Anti-Feminist
Educator
Native Rights Activist
Politician
Postmaster Muscogee
Social Worker
Teacher

Robertson was the second U.S. congresswoman and the first to defeat an incumbent congressman. She was the only woman to be elected to Congress from Oklahoma until 2006.

She opposed many women's groups.

She also voted against maternity and childcare legislation, thinking it gave the government too much power over personal rights. She voted against an anti-lynching bill.

On 20 June 1921 she was the first woman to hold the gavel as she presided over the House of Representatives.

She grew up on Creek Indian lands in Arkansas. Her first job was with the Bureau of Indian Affairs and she taught for two years at the Carlisle Indian Industrial School in Pennsylvania. She later taught at a school for Native American girls that became Tulsa University.

When she left Congress, she ran a dairy farm and a café.

225. Gertrud Emma Scholtz-Klink
Born 9 February 1902 Adelsheim, Germany
Died 24 March 1999 Tübingen Bebenhausen, Germany

Nazi Party Member
Politician

In complete contrast to those fighting for women's right, Scholtz-Klink's role as Reich's Women's *Füherin* was to enshrine women's role as a good *Hausfrau*.

As a Nazi party member, she was appointed leader of the Nazi Women's league by Adolf Hitler.

The mother of six children, before her first husband, a factory worker, left her a widow, she married Dr. Günther Scholtz. Six years later they divorced.

She fought against women in politics, although she was in politics. Male politicians paid her little heed. Schlotz-Klink was quoted as saying, "The mission of woman is to minister in the home and in her profession to the needs of life from the first to last moment of man's existence."

Women's organizations established programs to teach family and household management.

Her third husband was *SS-Obergruppenführer*, August Heissmeyer. At the end of the war, they hid near Tübingen but were arrested three years later. She was sentenced to over four years in prison.

PRISONER

According to Statista.com there were 87,784 women imprisoned in the United States, six times higher than in 1980. According to the Sentencing Project, 58% have a child under 18. Figures from the United Kingdom government, 87,216, weren't much different. The population of the United States was 339,665,118 and the United Kingdom population was 68,138,484 in September 2023.

226. Mimi Reinhardt
Born 15 January 1915 Vienna Neustadt, Austria
Died April 2022 Herzliya, Israel

Prisoner at the Plaszow camp
Secretary for Oskar Schlinder

Oskar Schlinder has received much recognition for saving Jews in World War II, as well he should. However, he was helped by his secretary within the camp, Mimi Reinhardt, who prepared the list of Jewish workers to be transferred to Brünnlitz subcamp to work in Schindler's armament factory.

Reinhardt was widowed at 30. Her husband had been shot trying to escape the Krakow ghetto. She and her husband were arrested; he was shot at the gate of the ghetto.

After the liquidation of the ghetto, she was transported with other Jews to Plaszow. Because she knew shorthand, she worked in camp administration, where she met Oskar Schindler.

She knew he treated his Jewish workers well. After Schindler had asked the SS camp commander for more workers, she typed lists of workers to be transferred to the Brünnlitz subcamp.

PROGRAMMER

Computer programmers create instructions so a computer can perform certain jobs.

In the beginning women dominated the field but lost their advantage after World War II. India has less of a gender gap in computing than other countries. About 25% of those in computing are women, although there have been/are women CEOs of tech companies.

227. Danielle "Dan" Bunten Berry
Born 19 February 1949 St. Louis, Missouri
Died 3 July 1998 Little Rock, Arkansas of lung cancer

Game Designer
Programmer

Berry began life as a man, transitioned to a woman, including surgery, although she expressed some regrets. She joked it was one way to increase the number of women in a male-dominated gaming industry.

As the oldest of six children, Burton loved playing games with her family. She became a leading creator of computer games including M.U.L.E, Wheeler Dealer and The Seven Cities of Gold.

While studying for an industrial engineering degree, she opened a bike shop. After her degree she went to work for National Science, followed by work at a video game company.

Finally, she founded Ozark Softscape, which operated out of her basement. Popularity of her games varied. Seven Cities was extremely popular, selling 150,000 copies.

PSYCHOLOGISTS

By 2017 women outnumbered men in the field of psychology in the United States. 64.8% of all psychologists are women, while 35.2% are men according to zippla.com.

228. Lou Andreas-Salomé
Born 12 February 1861 St. Petersburg, Russia
Died 5 February 1937 Gottingen, Germany of diabetes and heart problems

Psychoanalyst
Writer

Salomé lived her life on her own terms.

She was from a Huguenot family, the only girl with five brothers. She was educated as her brothers were leaning French, German and Russian. She became non-religious.

She was friends and lovers with some of the great thinkers of her time in the areas of art, poetry, philosophy and psychology.

Many proposed. She said no to philosopher Friedrich Nietzsche and writer Paul Ree. She remained friends with both men.

Problems with diabetes and her heart plagued her.

She wrote *Im Kampf um Gott* about the loss of faith. Besides fiction, she wrote about Friedrich Nietzsche, Freud and Rilke. Her relationship with Rilke was that of lover, friend, advisor and muse.

She worked as a psychoanalyst. The Nazis confiscated her library because of her connections with what was thought of as a "Jewish

Science."

229. Marie Louise von Franz
Born 4 January 1915 Munich, Germany
Died 17 February 1998 Küssnacht, Switzerland of Parkinson's
Disease

Jungian Psychologist
Scholar

Working closely as a psychologist with Carl Jung, Von Franz claimed to interpret 63,000 dreams. She had met Jung at age 18 when beginning her studies at Zurich University including classical philology, Latin, Greek, literature and ancient history. Family financial problems meant she had to support herself, which she did by tutoring.

After finishing her studies and working as an analyst, she wrote over 20 books, with an emphasis on the relationship of psychology and fairy tales, the first to do so. She said they were the "purest and simplest expression of collective unconscious psychic processes." One project took her nine years.

She also made a series of films, *The Way of the Dream*, which became an English TV series.

She was active as the librarian of the Psychology Club of Zurich and co-founder of the C.G. Jung Institute in Zurich.

She traveled widely and created a home in the woods lacking electricity and toilet facilities where she retreated to work while escaping civilization.

230. Alice Miller

Born 12 January 1923 Trybunalski, Poland
Died 14 April 2010 Saint-Rémy de Provence, France of suicide
after fighting pancreatic cancer

Psychologist
Philosopher

Miller was one of the first to write extensively about both physical
and psychological abuse of children. Her book, *The Drama of the
Gifted Child,* was an international bestseller in 1981. Contrary to the
popular idea childhood trauma was the fault of the child, she believed
it was the parent's responsibility, and she believed much violence in
adults can be traced to childhood abuse.

In 1939 she escaped the Trybunalski, Poland Jewish ghetto. Her
father died there.

Seven years later she was studying on a scholarship at Basel
University. Her Ph.D. was in philosophy, psychology and sociology.

She practiced psychoanalysis for 20 years in Zurich before
abandoning it as useless.

For the last five years she lived, she wrote articles and conducted
interviews.

She maintained a website and responded to readers.

Her 24-year marriage produced two children.

231. Judith Wallerstein
Born 27 December 1921 New York City, New York
Died 18 June 2012 Piedmont, California of an intestinal obstruction

Psychologist
Researcher
Writer

Wallerstein conducted a 25-year study on how children were affected by divorce. Her parents had not been divorced, but her father died from cancer when she was eight. She, herself, was not divorced but had a 65-year marriage. Some of her work was criticized because she worked mainly with middle-class, educated families.

Her research was based on 131 families with children between three and 18.

Academically she taught at the University of California, Berkeley, Hebrew University and Pahlavi University Iran, Harvard, Cornell, Stanford and Yale.

As founder of the Judith Wallerstein Center for the Family in Transition, she saw the center provided counseling for 60 couples and their children in the throes of divorce.

She wrote:
- *Second Chances, The Unexpected Legacy of Divorce*
- *What About the Kids*
- *The Good Marriage: How and Why Love Lasts*

She served on many committees and commissions.

REFORMERS

Reformers tackle problems and seek solutions. The problems can apply to almost any human activity. Women have often looked at problems and done whatever they can to solve them, often at great personal sacrifice.

232. Elisabeth Achelis
Born 11 January 1880 Brooklyn, New York
Died 11 February 1973 Brooklyn, New York in her sleep

Reformer for calendar change

Imagine living with an invariable calendar. There would be four Friday the 13s.

Thanksgiving would always be 23 November. One January would always be Sunday.

As an heir to the American Hard Rubber Company fortune, money was not a problem for Achelis, letting her work on her passion.

Her introduction to the idea of a twelve-month calendar with dates following on the same day of the week every year was her life's work.

The world calendar has four quarters of 91 days with each quarter beginning Sunday and ending Saturday. The quarters are equal: each has exactly 91 days, 13 weeks, or 3 months.

She founded The World Calendar Association (TWCA) to encourage worldwide adoption of the World Calendar.

The League of Nations supported the idea.

To promote the calendar, she published the *Journal of Calendar Reform* and wrote five books.

233. Mary Williams Dewson
Born 18 February 1874 Quincy, Massachusetts
Died 21 October 1962 Castine, Maine

Activist
Feminist
Reformer

This tomboy devoted her life to many related causes that made the world a better place for women. Her skills in gathering statistics helped justify her work.

A Wellesley College graduate, where she was senior class president, she held many activist roles in the National Consumers League and was civic Secretary of the Women's City Club of New York.

Her Reporter Plan encouraged women to promote New Deal legislation, bringing thousands of women into active civic participation.

When Eleanor Roosevelt encouraged Dewson to become a more active Democrat, she listened. She replaced Roosevelt as Women's Division Head of the Democratic National Campaign Committee.

During World War I she worked with the Red Cross in France.

She helped pass the first minimum wage law in Massachusetts.

Working with delinquent girls, she was helped by her statistical gathering skills in justifying her programs.

She wrote *The Twentieth Century Expense Book*, a guide on household budgeting.

234. Katharina von Bora Luther

Born 29 January 1499? Lippendorf? Electorate of Saxony, Holy Roman Empire

Died 20 December 1552 Torgau, Electorate of Saxony, Holy Roman Empire

Business Leader
Reformer
Religious Leader

As the wife of Martin Luther, she was said to be an influence for Protestant marriages especially with clerics. Tracing her influence can be difficult because of limited or confusing records.

She came from lesser Saxon nobility and was placed in a Benedictine convent at the age of five but four years later was moved to a Cistercian community where she became a nun which was not a good match. She is said to have asked Martinn Luther to help free her and her escape in a merchant's covered wagon was arranged for her and other nuns. This was considered a crime.

Her fellow nuns found jobs or husbands, but Katherina did not. She insisted on marrying Luther who agreed saying it "would please his father, rile the pope, cause the angels to laugh, and the devils to weep."

She became the manager of the monastery's holdings and increased profits. When Luther died, under Saxon law, she could not inherit his property, forcing her into poverty.

She fled the area during the Black Plague and was thrown into a ditch until removed. For three months, she hovered between life and death before succumbing.

RELIGIOUS LEADERS

Women have played a subordinate role in most of the world's major religions throughout history. Still, some became head of convents, wrote on spiritual subjects and started religious movements. Today there are glimmers of light in women assuming responsible positions in the major religions.

235. Agnes of Bohemia, O:S:C: (Agnes of Prague)

Born 20 January 1211 Prague Bohemia (Today Czech)

Died 2 March 1282 Prague, Bohemia (Czech)

Like many royal women throughout the ages, Agnes was a political pawn until she said enough is enough. Promised in marriage to the King of Germans at age eight, the contract was cancelled eight years later, leading to a war.

When there were ongoing maneuvers to marry her to other royalty, she decided to lead a religious life.

She asked Pope Gregory IX to help her devote her life to prayer. Emperor Frederick, one of the proposed husbands, is said to have stated: "If she had left me for a mortal man, I would have taken vengeance with the sword, but I cannot take offence because in preference to me she has chosen the King of Heaven."

On land donated by Agnes's brother, she founded two friaries and a hospital. She also had an active correspondence with Claire of Assis, who founded the Order of Poor Ladies.

236. Jeanne-Marie de La Motte-Guyon
Born 13 April 1648 Montargis, Orléanais
Died 9 June 1717 Blois, France

Heretic
Writer

After publishing a book about Quietism, a set of contemplative practices, Madame Guyon was imprisoned for seven years.

She'd been unhealthy during her childhood.

Her parents were extraordinarily religious. She was educated by nuns, often in convents. She considered becoming a nun.

At 15 a marriage with Jacques Guyon, age 38, was arranged by her parents.

After suffering the death of her family members, her husband and two of her five children, she believed that her suffering would mean she would be blessed.

She claimed three mystical experiences.

The Bishop of Geneva, with whom she later fought, encouraged her to establish a place near Geneva to convert Protestants. Guyon fought with the nuns in the house. She was asked to leave both Geneva then Grenoble, because of her ideas.

She divested herself of property with the exception of one annuity.

The first of two arrests led to her imprisonment. Upon release she lived with a son and continued promoting her beliefs.

237. Alice Marie Jourdain Hildebrand
Born 11 March 1923 Brussels, Belgium
Died 14 January New Rochelle, New York

Author
Catholic philosopher
Professor
Theologian

Von Hildebrand struggled to find employment in academia but finally was able to teach philosophy at Hunter College, which she did for 37 years. Prior to that, she'd been rejected by Catholic colleges, who informed her that they did not employ women to teach philosophy. Even then, it took 14 years to gain tenure at Hunter.

Hunter's president tried to convince her she would be better teaching at a Catholic college, which was contrary to her opinion that it was important for a Catholic to be at a secular school.

She married German Roman Catholic philosopher and religious writer Dietrich von Hildebrand and launched the Dietrich von Hildebrand Legacy Project. Her biography of her husband, *The Soul of a Lion: The Life of Dietrich von Hildebran,* was published in 2000.

Memoirs of a Happy Failure documents her escape from Nazi Europe.

238. Marguerite Porete
Born 13th Century, Holy Roman Empire
Died 1 June 1310 Paris, France burned at the stake

Mystic

Porete wrote *The Mirror of Simple Souls,* a book about divine love that is of interest to medieval mysticism and medieval women's writing.

The book was written sometime in the 1290s. That it was written in Old French rather than the Latin was used against her during her trial for heresy.

Facts about her life are skimpy. What is known, she claimed she had shown the book to a church official. However, she was said to have been arrested in Châlons-en-Champagne in 1308 and held in a prison for 18 months before her trial. During her arrest and trial, she refused to cooperate with any of her inquisitors.

Three bishops pronounced her guilty. It was said that the crowd witnessing her burning cried.

239. Susanna Wesley
Born 20 January 1669 London, England
Died 23 July 1742 London, England

Religious Leader

Susanna (Annesley) Wesley was the 25th of 25 children. She was an early dissenter from her father's church and joined the Church of England. She married Samuel Wesley at age 19. They had 19 children. Only eight survived.

Her life was not easy. Her husband left her temporarily. Money was hard to come by. Wesley was upset at their lack of discipline. They lost two homes to fire. Her children were farmed out during the rebuilding.

She made sure her children were well educated and that included learning Latin and Greek.

When her husband was away, she ran family services, often attended by up to 200 people. Her afternoon services were more popular than her husband's morning ones.

She was the mother of Charles Wesley, who wrote over 6,000 hymns, and John Wesley, the founder of the Methodist movement within the Church of England. Susanna has been called the "Mother of the Methodist Movement."

RESISTANCE FIGHTERS

Resistance fighters in a war risked their lives to overthrow their enemies or occupiers. In this selection we list World War II resistance fighters, although from a German perspective of the time they would be considered terrorists or traitors. The main requirement of a resistance fighter is unbelievable bravery and the willingness to take risks far above normal.

240. Jeanette Guyot
Born 26 February 1919 Chalon sur Saöne, France
Died 10 April 2016 Sevrey, France

Resistance Fighter
Spy

Guyot followed her parents into the French resistance during World II. Her many missions included accompanying fugitives from Nazi-occupied territory to safety in the Vichy section of France.

At one point she installed a radio next door to a Nazi office.

In February 1942, she was caught by the Germans. Three months later she was released. Her parents were unlucky and were sent to a concentration camp.

Because Guyot was in danger herself, the Royal Air Force picked her up in central France and took her to safety.

For several months she worked with the Free French Forces in London and later with the Secret Intelligence Service and Office of Strategic Service.

In February 1944 she and two others were parachuted into occupied France. Their assignment was to find drop zones and safe houses.

After the war, she was reunited with her mother. Her father had died in Germany.

She married another agent, Marcel Gaucher, and lived a relatively normal life.

241. Irena Stanisława Sendler
Born 15 February 1910 Warsaw, Poland
Died 12 May 2008 Warsaw, Poland

Humanitarian
Nurse
Resistance Fighter (Polish Underground)

With the help of others, Sendler smuggled 2000+ Jewish children out of the Warsaw ghetto, providing them with fake documents. From early in the war, she had smuggled food into the ghetto for those that couldn't get out.

Some children were hidden in coffins, potato sacks, underground tunnels or ambulances. Others entered the Jewish side of a Catholic church that straddled the ghetto boundary and left on the other side with new identities.

Sendler then helped place the children in convents, orphanages or with non-Jewish families. They were taught Christian doctrine and prayers so if caught, they would be able to respond correctly.

She made records of the children's names but even under torture, she would not give the Gestapo any information about their whereabouts.

Most of the children's parents were killed.

She did this work for three years until her arrest by the Gestapo in October 1943. Using bribery, she escaped her death sentence.

242. Cecile Pearl Witherington Cornioley
Born 24 June 1914 Paris, France
Died 24 February 2008 Châteauvieux, France

Resistance Fighter
Secret Agent
Secretary

The daughter of a British couple, Witherington was born in France. She had the code names Marie and Pauline and was an effective agent in France for the United Kingdom's clandestine Special Operations Executive (SOE) in World War II.

She was parachuted into France to meet with Resistance cells with whom she worked, some 2000 fighters of the Wrestler group part of the *maquisard* fighters. Their missions included dropping weapons and blowing up targets.

The Germans, who suffered great damage as the result of the Resistance, offered a reward of one million francs for her capture. In May 1944, she was captured and sent to Buchenwald concentration camp.

Witherington was one of the few secret agents to survive the camp.

REVOLUTIONARIES

Unlike resistance fighters, revolutionaries may or not fight for their causes during a war but during peace time as well. A revolutionary is someone who wants rapid change from the status quo whether in politics, science, or any field.

243. Catherine Breshkovsky
Born 25 January 1844 Ivanova, Russia
Died 12 September 1934 Chvaly, Czechoslovakia

Revolutionary
Socialist

She's been called the Babushka, the grandmother of the Revolution.

As Russia's first female political prisoner, Breshkovsky was a major contributor to the Russian socialist movement. As a young woman, she helped her father, a noble, free the family serfs and saw that they were educated.

She married a landowner, had a son, but left him with relatives for years, as she pursued her causes.

Her activities resulted in her being in and out of prisons/exile most of her early adult life.

In 1903 she escaped to Geneva, Switzerland, then traveled to the U.S. to give talks. Nearly 3,000 people gave her a standing ovation when she spoke in Boston, Massachusetts. She raised $10,000 for her cause, returning to Russia for the 1905 revolution.

To escape her 1910 life sentence in Siberia she rode on horseback

600+ miles before being captured and put into solitary confinement for two years.

After the 1917 Revolution she was freed and became a member of the Constituent Assembly, its oldest member. She helped form the Socialist-Revolutionary Party.

244. Lil Milagro de la Esperanza Ramírez Huezo Córdoba
Born 3 April 1946 Essa, San Salvador, El Salvador
Murdered in jail17 October 1979 San Salvado, El Salvador

Poet
Revolutionary Leader

A poet and revolutionary, Lil Milagro, was tortured in prison before being shot.

As a doctoral student at El Salvador University, she had refused to graduate. She did not want to be part of an unjust political system.

She moved from Christian Socialism to embracing some of Karl Marx's teachings. By 1971 she was part of El Grupo. It morphed into the People's Revolutionary Army (ERP), but in 1975 she and others supported Resistencia Nacional (RN).

She was captured in November 1976 by Guardia Nacional (GN) and she was shot in the head, but survived, then was taken to the Customs Police where she was subjected to truth serum and held in inhumane conditions until she was murdered.

The Salvadoran Civil War was ended by the Chapultepec Peace Accords signed 16 January 1992.

245. Haydée Santamaría Cuadrado

Born 30 December 1922, Constancia, Encrucijada, Villa Clara, Cuba
Died 28 July 1980 Havana, Cuba

Communist
Politician
Revolutionary
Teacher

She was a member of the Cuban Revolution from start to finish as a founder of the Communist Party of Cuba and in its ongoing leadership.

Her education was stopped at 6th grade because of family finances. Although she could not become a nurse as she wanted, she was able to teach for a short time.

She was one of two women fighting in the Moncada Barack in the July 1953 attack and was imprisoned for her part, which included procuring weapons.

After her release, she was one of the 26th of July Movement founders, much of which was done in Miami, Florida.

She was part of the guerrilla forces led by Fidel Castro and Che Guevara. She was a member of the all-woman Mariana Grajales Platoon, Castro's security group.

246. Mairéad Farrell
Born 3 March 1957 Belfast, Northern, Ireland
Died 6 March 1988 Gibraltar, shot

Revolutionary/Irish Patriot

Farrell, Sean Savage and Daniel McCann were killed by the British Army in Gibraltar during Operation Flavius, which was trying to stop an IRA bombing. The deaths were ruled "lawful killings," which the families took to the European Court of Human Rights, who ruled they had been "unlawfully killed."

Although her family were not militant Irish Republicans, Farrell joined the Provisional IRA at age 14. She fought against British rule almost all her adult life.

In March 1976, she tried to bomb a hotel where British soldiers on temporary duty stayed.

She was arrested: her boyfriend was shot.

At her trial she refused to recognize the jurisdiction of the British court. She was sent to Armagh, primarily a woman's prison, where 33 Republican women were imprisoned.

During her imprisonment, she refused to wear the prison uniform. Other rebellious acts included smearing feces and menstrual blood on the walls and a hunger strike.

After her release in October 1986, she studied Political Science and Economics at Queen's University but left to continue working with the IRA.

247. Vera Nikolayevna Figner Filippova

Born 7 July 1852 Kazan Governorate, Russia
Died 25 June 1942 Moscow, Russia of natural causes

Activist
Revolutionary
Writer

Born into a noble family of German and Russian descent, Figner was a leader of the clandestine *Narodnaya Volya* (People's Will) group, which believed in terror to achieve a revolutionary overthrow of the government.

Figner helped plan the successful assassination of Alexander II of Russia in 1881 for which she was arrested and spent 20 months in solitary confinement prior to trial. She was given a death sentence which was later commuted, but she spent 20 years in the Shlisselburg Fortress. On release she was exiled.

Figner gained international fame in large part because of the widely translated memoir of her experiences. She was treated as a heroic icon of revolutionary sacrifice after the 1917 February Revolution and was a popular public speaker during that year.

She later became prominent in the Society of Former Political Prisoners and Exiles in the Soviet Union until its dissolution in 1935.

248. Heloise Ruth First
Born 4 May 1925 Johannesburg, South Africa
Assassinated 17 August 1982 Maputo, Mozambique by a parcel
bomb

Activist
Communist
Journalist
Revolutionary

First was the first woman held under the Ninety-Day Detention
Law, spending 117 days in isolation for anti-apartheid activities. She
would fight for her causes all her life.

She was the daughter of Latvian Jewish emigrants to South Africa.
Her parents were founding members of the South African Communist
Party. First joined as well. The Party aligned with the African National
Congress and the goal of overthrowing the government.

At Witwatersrand University she helped found the Progressive
Students League.

The paper *The Guardian*, where she was editor-in-chief, was banned.
It helped expose apartheid policies by the National Party.

She rioted in the 1950s.

With her husband, Joe Slovo, the couple continued to protest.

She stood trial starting in 1956 but was not acquitted for four years.
Later she was imprisoned and spent 117 days in isolation.

Exiled to London, she taught and continued anti-apartheid
activities.

A member of the South African Police, Craig Williamson, ordered
her assassination.

249. Vilma Lucila Espín Guillois
Born 7 April 1930 Santiago, Cuba
Died 18 June 2007 Havana, Cuba after a long illness

Chemical Engineer
Feminist
Revolutionary¨
Spy

Throughout her childhood, Guillois was an excellent student in math, chemistry and physics. Her father tried to discourage her from socialist activities while encouraging her to go to M.I.T. as the first Cuban woman to study chemical engineering. She did, but it only increased her animosity to the United States.

Going back home via Mexico she joined the 26th of July Movement as a spy and in opposition to dictator Fulgencio Batista and became a revolutionary leader.

She founded Federation of Cuban Women, a group that passed a law that men must help women with household chores. She also worked to improve women's educational opportunities as she fought for women's issues such as abortion.

In 1976 at the National Assembly of People's Power she was elected deputy and member of the State Council.

250. Fanny Efimovna Kaplan (Feiga Haimovna)
Born 10 February 1890 Volhynian Governorate, Russie
Executed 3 September 1918 Moscow, Russia by bullet

Attempted Assassin
Milliner
Revolutionary

Kaplan shot at Vladimir Lenin three times as he left a factory on 30 August 1918. Two bullets wounded him, but he recovered.

She admitted she shot him, calling him a traitor to the Revolution.

Of Jewish descent, there are few known details of her early life, except she was home educated and had worked as a milliner. She was considered to be a Socialist-Revolutionary and Soviet dissident.

In 1906, she was arrested when she was accused of having participated in a bomb plot and was subsequently imprisoned in a labor camp. Beatings and mistreatment led to partial loss of her sight. She was released in 1917 after the Tsar's overthrow.

Unhappy with non-Bolsheviks being in control, she took self-action.

Some reports questioned her mental stability. Other reports say she admitted firing the shots. There are also reports that a bullet recovered from Lenin did not come from Kaplan's gun.

On 3 September 1918, Kaplan was shot, and her body burned.

251. Musine Kokalari
Born 10 February 1917 Adana, Ottoman Empire
Died 14 August 1983 Rrëshen, Albania of breast cancer

Anti-Fascist
Communist Dissident
Revolutionary
Writer

"Musine was one of the first intellectuals who sacrificed her comfort for the benefit of democracy," according to the Musine Kokalari Institute, a think tank promoting social democratic values.

Although her family moved several times, she grew up surrounded by books and music.

Her literary studies were in Rome.

At 20, she began publishing on social policy issues. One of the first Albanian published writers, her first book, *As The Old Woman Told Me,* was only published in 1941. Her work attracted the interest of other writers.

Her writing was banned by the Albanian Communist government.

Her activities led to her arrest on 23 January 1946 by Enver Hoxa's government. She was sentenced to 30 years. It was later reduced to 20. Her two brothers were shot without trial two years before.

After her release she found work as a streetsweeper, forbidden to write.

252. Sybil (or Sibbell) Ludington
Born 5 April 1761 Fredericksburg, New York
Died 26 February 1839 Unadilla, New York

Revolutionary?

Was she a heroine of the American Revolutionary War or not?

The story goes that on 26 April 1777, the 16-year-old rode 40 miles on her horse, maybe named Star, to warn the countryside of the British, who had just burned Danbury, Connecticut. Her ride was designed to help rally 400 local militia.

True or not, she became a heroine complete with historic road markers along her route.

The story arose from 1907 memoirs about her father, Militia Colonel Henry Ludington, which were published privately.

Historian Martha Lamb claimed that her evidence about Sybil's ride came from letters, sermons and other documents, none of which she cited.

The Daughters of American Revolution said, "It's a great story, but there is no way to know whether or not it is true."

253. Constance Georgine Booth Markievicz
Born 4 February 1868 London, England
Died 15 July 1927 Dublin, Ireland with complications from
appendicitis surgery

Irish politician
Nationalist
Painter
Revolutionary
Suffragist

Despite her London birth, Markievicz joined the 1916 Irish Easter
Rising to overthrow British Rule. Her job was recruiting people to
peel potatoes. Her father, Sir Henry, had provided potatoes to the
Irish during the famine at his cost.

She was imprisoned and sentenced to death, commuted to life
imprisonment because she was a woman. While in prison, she was
the first woman elected to the UK House of Commons.

As part of party policy, she refused her seat.

Instead, she, with other Sinn Féin MPs, formed the first Dáil
Éireann and continued as a Sinn Fein Dáil member until 1926.

Her revolutionary activities contrasted with her early desire to be a
painter and despite her family's shock, she studied at London's Slade
School of Art. In Paris while studying at the Académie Julian, she
met her husband Casimir Markievicz. Both of the couple were from
wealthy families. They settled in Dublin.

254. Marie-Jeanne 'Manon' Roland de la Platière
Born 17 March 1754 Paris, France
Executed 8 November 1793 Paris, France

Revolutionary
Writer

She said she would have preferred to live in Roman times. Despite being frustrated by the lack of women's opportunities, she became an important voice promoting the French Revolution, although much of what she wrote was under her husband's name.

Daughter of a successful businessman, she was home schooled. She did not win a prize in a contest with her essay, "How the education of women can help make men better."

Her husband and she joined the French Revolutionary elite protesting social conditions. She moved from wanting social reform to believing in civil war.

The couple were associated with the Girondins and Jacobins to end the monarchy, but the groups had philosophical differences. Ideas were often discussed in her salons, which attracted leading thinkers.

In Spring 1792 she proposed establishing an army camp of 20,000 men outside Paris.

After the king was overthrown, the Reign of Terror made the couple's position dangerous.

She was arrested twice, tried and beheaded while wearing a yellow and white muslin dress.

255. Pritilata Waddedar

Born 5 May 1911 Dhalghat, Patiya, Chittagong, Bengal
Suicide 24 September 1932 suicide by cyanide

Revolutionary

Waddedar has been called "Bengal's first woman martyr." She was an influencer in the drive for Indian independence.

She came from a middle-class family where education was important. A graduate in philosophy, she taught school and espoused the importance of nationalism.

She joined a group led by revolutionary leader Surya Kumar Sen.

She led 15 fellow revolutionaries in a 1932 armed attack on a European club that had a sign "Dogs and Indians not allowed." For the assault she wore men's clothing. About 40 people were inside and the attackers divided themselves into three groups. One woman died, eleven were injured.

Waddedar, rather than be arrested, took the cyanide pill provided by the revolutionary group.

SAILOR

Until the 20th century, ships were the only method of transportation across a body of water. Throughout history the majority of sailors were men with women the rare exception.

According to Wikipedia 69,629 were in the U.S. Navy in 1920. Of those 11,076 were officers. Women's first roles in the navy were as nurses going back as far as the Civil War. However, unlike men they had to provide for their own housing and food. Zippa reports only 11% of the merchant marines are comprised of women. Women might work on private ships, but that too was rare.

256. Mary Ann Brown Patten
Born 6 April 1837 Chelsea, Massachusetts
Died 18 March 1861 Massachusetts of tuberculosis

Merchant commander of a clipper ship

Nineteen-year-old Patten was pregnant when she survived a mutiny to take over her husband's clipper ship *Neptune's Car* after he collapsed. She was the first woman to command an American merchant vessel.

Patten had taught herself navigation during a trip and assisted her captain husband in his duties.

Mary became the most qualified on board when her husband was incapacitated. The ship arrived safely in San Francisco. She claimed she didn't change clothes as she commanded the ship and took care of her ailing husband.

Two other ships were racing on the New York to San Francisco trip and bets were placed.

The first mate wanted to put into a South American port, tried to convince the rest of the crew, but Patten won them over.

In San Francisco, Patten refused to be replaced.

Both she and her husband died of tuberculosis.

SCIENTISTS

More studies are being done on the number of women in STEM (science, technology, engineering and math) jobs. Women are still underrepresented in all STEM fields. In history, women's participation in science was hampered by them not having access to education in countries around the world. A few succeeded.

257. Marian Ewurama Addy
Born 7 February 1942 Nkawkaw, Ghana
Died 14 January 2014 Accra, Ghana natural causes

Biochemist

A full professor, a quiz show host and a researcher in herbal medicine safety and efficiency for allergies and diabetes are three of the areas where Dr. Addy stood out, making her a role model for young girls thinking of careers in technology, the sciences and/or math.

The quiz show was her way to encourage secondary students to look at the sciences as a career. Her studies at Ghana University in botany and chemistry were followed at Pennsylvania State University where she earned a Ph.D. in biochemistry.

In January 2008, Addy became President of the Anglican University College of Technology.

She worked with many organizations and agencies in various capacities. To name a few:
- Policy Committee on Developing Countries (PCD.C.)
- National Board for Professional and Technicians

Examinations (NABPTEX)
- Science Education Programme for Africa (SEPA)
- National Council for Tertiary Education (NCTE)

258. Ana Aslan
Born 1 January 1897 Braila, Romania
Died 20 May 1988 Bucharest, Romania

Biologist
Doctor specialist in gerontology

Aslan went on a hunger strike to convince her mother she should go to medical school. The mother was a widow with four children and the reasons she objected were financial and being a doctor was not considered a desirable pursuit for a woman.

Aslan nursed soldiers during World War I before graduating in 1924 with a degree in cardiovascular physiology. Her interests focused on ageing. She discovered the effect procaine had on arthritis.

A three-year study led to the development of Gerovital (H3). Future studies involved 15,000 people with strong results.

Working in 1976 with pharmacist Elena Polovrăgeanu, they invented Aslavital to delay the skin aging process. She was director of the National Institute of Geriatrics and Gerontology from 1958 until 1988.

259. Alice Augusta Ball
Born 24 July 1892 Seattle, Washington
Died 31 December 1916 Hawaii

Chemist

The discovery of the Ball Method to treat previously untreatable leprosy was usurped by her advisor Arthur L. Dean after Ball's death.

Her Masters degree, which she received from Hawaii University, was the first given to a woman and first African American.

She received two degrees from Washington University: one in pharmaceutical chemistry and the other in pharmacy science. She and her advisor, William Dehn, co-published a 10-page paper, "Benzoylations in Ether Solution," unheard for a woman of any ethnic background.

Because of her knowledge of plant chemical makeup, she was offered a post with the U. S. Public Health Service in Leprosy Investigation Station to study the leprosy treatment with Chaulmoogra oil, which had certain problems. Ball's technique to make the oil injectable and water-soluble solved the problems of blisters and vomiting from the oil.

It wasn't until 1922 when she received credit for the method, which had been called the Dean Method.

Her death was recorded as tuberculosis but may have been caused by exposure to chlorine in the laboratory.

260. Alice Eastwood
Born 19 January 1859 Toronto, Canada
Died 30 October 1953 San Francisco, California

Botanist

To prove a degree is not always necessary to be an expert, Eastwood taught herself botany from manuals and other sources. Her knowledge and collections led to a position at the California Academy of Sciences herbarium. Eastwood was made procurator and head of the Department of Botany in 1894.

She built its botanical collection.

Not only did she publish over 310 scientific articles, she named 395 land plant species.

Her work was not limited to the herbarium. She made trips to areas that were wildernesses as well as to other countries.

She saved 1,497 plant types from the 1906 San Francisco earthquake and fires by using her apron to lower plants from a window from the damaged building.

She rebuilt the lost collection.

261. Gertrude "Trudy" Belle Elion
Born 23 January 1918 New York, New York
Died 21 February 1999 Chapel Hill, North Carolina

Biochemist
Pharmacologist
Secretary
Teacher

Elion fought gender bias during her early life. Her gender prohibited Elion from getting financial aid for graduate school and a job. She went to secretarial school and later worked as a secretary and teacher and finally in a chemistry lab without pay.

She was not allowed to continue graduate studies at the future Brooklyn Polytechnic Institute as a part time student. She decided on her job over studying for a Ph.D., but in 1989 she was awarded an honorary doctorate.

When her fiancé died from bacterial endocarditis, his loss reinforced her commitment to research.

After working for several cancer research groups and the World Health Organization, she joined Burroughs Wellcome until her retirement in 1983. After retirement she continued research combining it with travel and support of other women who wanted to pursue a scientific career.

Her work contributed to the development of drugs used against AIDS, leukemia and herpes.

She also developed drugs to fight against rejection in organ transplants.

262. Eloise "Elo" R. Giblett
Born 17 January 1921 Tacoma, Washington
Died 16 September 2009 Seattle, Washington

Genetic scientist
Hematologist

Dr. Giblett's mother, it was said, wanted her to be the next Shirley Temple, focusing her daughter's early education on singing, dancing and violin.

Dr. Giblett was more interested in science. At University of Washington Medical School, where she was one of five women, she graduated first in her class.

After her internship and residency in internal medicine at King

County Hospital, a two-year fellowship led her into hematology research starting in 1953.

Over her career, she wrote 200+ research papers and a textbook, *Genetic Markers in Human Blood.* Her discoveries included the first recognized immunodeficiency disease and identifying blood group antigens.

She was an early supporter of bone marrow donations. Her research assisted in refuting the standard practice of segregating blood donations by race of the donor. She developed a blood screening process.

Upon retirement, she played the violin and worked with musical groups, a return to childhood interests.

She is mentioned in Robert Heinlein's novel *The Number of the Beast.*

263. Josephine Ettel Kablick
Born 9 March 1787 Vrchlabí, Czech
Died 21 July 1863 Ju Vrchlabí, Czech

Botanist
Paleontologist

From an early age and throughout her life, Kablick collected plants and fossils for museums, schools and her own herbarium. She ventured into difficult areas regardless of weather and circumstances. Her specimens numbered over 25,000.

She worked with other women and encouraged accurate drawings of what she discovered.

Botany was a field considered acceptable for women to work by many men. Her husband Adalbert Kablik, a pharmacologist and zoologist, supported her work.

She became a member of the Botanical Society in Vienna, the only woman to be allowed to join. Her admission to the Regensburgische Botanische Gesellschaft was only after the objections of another member were overcome.

She held a Ph.D.

Her work as a paleontologist was also recognized in her own time. Many of her discoveries have been named for her.

264. Kathleen Lonsdale
Born 28 January 1903 New Bridge, Ireland
Died 1 April 1971 London, England of anaplastic cancer

Crystallographer
Pacifist
Prison Reformer

Lonsdale used ping pong balls to demonstrate some of her research in crystallography, which determined the arrangement of atoms in crystalline solids. She also applied her research to kidney and gall stones.

She accomplished firsts for women including:
- First female professor at University College London
- First woman president of the International Union of Crystallography
- First woman president of the British Association for the Advancement of Science

She had attended Ilford County High School for Boys because the girls school did not offer the science and math courses she wanted. Her abilities were confirmed when she scored the highest grades in physics that a student ever had.

A move to Leeds meant she left her job, but she continued her research after her marriage, while staying home. Her husband, Thomas Lonsdale, a textile chemist, was supportive.

265. Ruth Sager
Born 7 February 1918 Chicago, Illinois
Died 29 March 1997 Brookline, Massachusetts of bladder cancer

Apple Farmer
Geneticist
Secretary
Writer

Dr. Sager adapted her career several times to her changing research interests. She enrolled in liberal arts at Chicago University but switched to mammalian physiology. When she was at Rutgers University, she studied plant physiology, concentrating on tomato seedling growth.

Following the war, she received her Ph.D. in maize genetics from Columbia University.

Until Dr. Sager, no one had published genetic mapping of a cellular organelle.

She published two books: *Cell Heredity*, co-authored with Frances Ryan, and *Cytoplasmic Genes and Organelles*.

During World War II she worked as an apple farmer and secretary.

She created the field of cytoplasmic genetics. It wasn't until the 1970s that her research was given the recognition it deserved.

Sager changed her research focus to cancer biology in the 1970s, with a specific focus on breast cancer, concentrating on the molecular and genetic cause, identifying over 100 possible tumor suppressor genes.

Dr. Sager was the recipient of a medal from the National Academy of Sciences.

266. Maria Emilie Snethlage
Born 13 April 1868 Brandenburg, Germany
Died 25 November 1929 Porto Velho, Brazil of a heart attack

Educator
Ornithologist

When Snethlage went to Berlin University at age 30, she had to arrive in class ahead of others and sit behind a screen. After class, she had to wait 15 minutes before leaving. She was already qualified to teach; she taught in England, Ireland and Germany.

The book, *Entdeckungsreisen in Feld und Flur,* read when she was young, stimulated her interest in nature. She began collecting plants and sharing her notes on birds to German ornithologist Rudolf Blasius.

She received a Ph.D. summa cum laude from Freiburg University. Her thesis was on insect musculature.

Her research took her to Brazil where she became director of the research center and museum called the *Museu Paraense Emílio Goeldi.* She was the first woman to head up a scientific center.

On one expedition she was on a boat, put her hand in the water and was bitten by a piranha. After it became infected, she self-amputated with a machete.

She collected thousands of specimens and recorded 45 new birds.

267. Evelyn M. Witkin
Born 9 March 1921 New York, New York
Died 8 July 2023 Plainsboro Township, New Jersey from
complications after a fall

Civil Rights Protestor
Geneticist

"A woman in the lab. This should be interesting," Theodosius
Dobzhansky responded when Witkin knocked on his door to ask to
become a graduate student at Columbia University.

She had been suspended and denied being valedictorian at New
York University because of her protests for Leonard Bates, a black
football player. The university left black football players at home
when the team played in the south.

Dobzhansky arranged for her to do her thesis research at Cold
Spring Harbor, known for its bacteria genetics research. After earning
her Ph.D., she spent another 11 years there.

Throughout her career she worked either alone or with a small
team, her preference.

Her groundbreaking work in DNA damage research resulted in a
greater understanding of the effects of aging and the causes of human
illnesses.

Witkin held two posts at Rutgers: Professor of Biological Sciences
at Douglass College and later at the Waksman Institute.

SEAMSTRESSES

Sewing was always thought of as a woman's job and responsibility. Dressmakers were usually women, but the top designers and tailors were men.

268. Ida Holdgreve
Born 1881 Delphos, Ohio
Died 1983 Lima, Ohio

Aerospace Worker
Seamstress

A typo of the word "plain" when it should have been "plane" was why Holdgreve answered an ad for "Plain Sewing Wanted." The Wright brothers were searching for someone to sew the cover for their fuselage.

The 29-year-old got the job despite disapproval of women working in factories. She was the only woman of 80 employees building 120 airplanes. A change from her previous work as a seamstress, she needed special training to make sure the cloth could be pulled tight.

Part of her job was to mend holes.

When the Wrights sold their company, she went with the purchaser, Dayton-Wright Airplane Company, but as a supervisor of other seamstresses.

During World War I, Dayton-Wright produced combat planes. Holdgreve was described as "Rosie the Riveter before there were airplane rivets." Her work after the war was making draperies in a store.

In 1969 she took her first flight.

269. Esther Steinberg Gluck

Born 11 January 1914 Veretsky, Austria-Hungary
Died c. 4 September 1942 Auschwitz, Poland

Seamstress

A found postcard was why the story of Esther Steinberg Gluck is known.

Only a few Irish Jews were killed in the Holocaust. Gluck was one of them.

Her family had moved to Dublin, Ireland in 1925. She worked as a seamstress.

She married Vogtjeck Gluck, a Belgian. They moved to Antwerp. With the Nazi threat looming they moved to Paris but feeling that was not safe they applied for Northern Ireland visas which arrived the day after the couple and their son, Leon, were caught by the Nazis and trained to Auschwitz.

Steinberg was able to write a postcard to her family and threw it from the train. "Uncle Lechem, we did not find, but we found Uncle Tisha B'Av." Also it said, "We did not find bread, but we found destruction." A stranger found the postcard and posted it. The family was put to death in September 1942.

SECRETARIES

The Administrative Professional Day began in 1952 under the auspices of the International Association of Administrative Professionals to recognize the work of secretaries and administrative assistants. It was an outgrowth of the National Secretaries Association. When women were able to enter the work force, they replaced men who served as the support to management until they dominated the profession. Computers have changed much of the work done by secretaries. Along with nurse and teacher, secretarial work was one of the few jobs available to women up until the late 20th century.

270. Hermine "Miep" Gies
Born 15 February 1909 Vienna, Austria
Died 11 January 2010 Hoorn, Netherlands from injuries in a fall

Accountant
Secretary

Almost everyone knows about Anne Frank, but less is known about Gies, who helped hide the Frank family during the Nazi occupation. She was also the woman who saved Anne Frank's diary.

She had been a foster child with a family who helped her through frail health. She was an excellent student and described as reserved and independent.

Having moved to the Netherlands, she worked for Otto Frank, who also had moved from Germany to escape the Nazis. She grew close to the Frank family. Her language skills helped them navigate

Dutch-language circles.

Her passport was revoked when she refused to join a woman's Nazi group.

To feed the Frank family, she went to several shops using illegally obtained ration cards provided by her husband and only carried one shopping bag.

After the Franks's arrest she tried to buy their freedom. It failed.

She returned Anne's papers after the war ended to Otto Frank.

SLAVES

Slavery is the ownership of a human being and having total control over their lives. The United States was not alone in considering slavery to be legal. It was a major issue in the mid-19th century and used as a reason for the Civil War. Slavery today is known as human trafficking.

271. Harriet Jacobs
Born c1813 or 1815 Edenton, North Carolina
Died 7 March 1897 Washington D.C.

Slave
Teacher
Writer

Jacobs wrote *Incidents in the Life of a Slave Girl* under the name Linda Brent. It was published in 1861.

Her mother was enslaved to a tavern owner. Technically her mother had been freed by a previous owner, but she had been kidnapped and returned to slavery. From age six, when her mother died, she lived with her mother's owner, a tavern keeper. When he died, she was given to his daughter, who taught her to read and write.

When sexually harassed by a new owner who threatened to sell her children if she did not give in, she hid in a crawl space under her grandmother's house for seven years until she could escape north where she was eventually reunited with her son, daughter and brother.

The man she worked for paid off her previous owner and legal fees to free her legally.

After the Civil War she went south and founded two schools to teach freed slaves reading and writing.

272. Bethany Veney
Born c. 1812–1815 Luray, Virginia
Died 16 November 1915 Worcester, Massachusetts

Slave
Writer

During one slave auction, Bethany Veney put baking soda in her mouth to appear sick. She would be sold and resold several times.

Veney, who also had Blackfoot Indian blood, wrote her autobiography, *Aunt Betty's Story: The Narrative of Bethany Veney, A Slave Woman*, which she dictated to M.W.G., a white woman.

She suffered abuse. One of her owners was considered "kind" because he fed and clothed them. At one point she was whipped with a nail rod leaving her lame.

Her first husband was a slave, her second was free. She met him when she cooked for his construction crew.

In December 1858, Veney and her son were sold for $775. Her purchaser freed her. As a free woman and after moving to Massachusetts, she would earn her living selling bluing and taking in washing.

Religion provided her with emotional strength. At a Methodist camp meeting she prayed for freedom. In Boston in 1867, she helped found African Methodist Episcopal Bethel Church.

She was able to move her family from the south and bought a home in Worcester, Massachusetts, living her final years as a free woman.

SOCIALISTS

Socialism can provoke horror or approval depending on the country and person who hears the word. Merriman-Webster defines it as "any of various egalitarian economic and political theories or movements advocating collective or governmental ownership and administration of the means of production and distribution of goods." Whether it is good, bad or something in between depends on how it is applied.

273. Marina Ginestà i Coloma
Born 29 January 1919 Toulouse, France
Died 6 January 2014 Paris, France

Journalist
Socialist

Coloma is more famous for her photograph than for herself. In it she stands on the rooftop of a Barcelona hotel holding a M1893 Spanish Mauser and wearing an army uniform on 21 July 1936 during the uprising. It has become a symbol for conflict.

She came from a leftist family.

After moving to Barcelona, she joined the Unified Socialist Party of Catalonia. When war started in 1936, she worked as a reporter and translator for *Pravda*.

After being wounded, she was taken to Montpellier but moved to the Dominican Republic where she married a Republican officer.

Under dictator Rafael Trujillo, she was prosecuted. She ran first to Venezuela then continued changing countries. By 1978 she had settled in Paris.

She said of the famous photo: "It's a good photo. It reflects the feeling we had at that moment. Socialism had arrived, the hotel guests had left. There was euphoria. We retired in Columbus, we ate well, as if bourgeois life belonged to us and we would have changed category quickly."

274. Adelheid Dworschak Popps
Born 11 February 1869 Inzersdorf, Austria
Died 7 March 1939 Vienna, Austria from stroke complications

Domestic Worker
Factory Worker
Feminist
Journalist
Politician
Seamstress Apprentice
Socialist

A housing development for the unemployed was named for her, a testimony to her work.

With a rocky and poor childhood and only three years of education, she had to support her family.

Often, she was sexually harassed.

After attending a meeting of the Social Democratic Workers Party as the only woman, she became one of their speakers and delegates. Her speeches included demands for women's education.

She became editor-in-chief of the social women's newspaper. She led a strike for women's clothing workers.

Both her sons from her marriage died.

She pushed to require women's votes in any party decisions.

Women weren't allowed in trade unions, thus denied a voice. She fought by creating the Union of Homeworkers and Association of Social Democratic Women and Girls.

Locally, she was elected to the Vienna Council and nationally to the Austrian Parliament.

Many of her ideas were lost in the male-dominated parliament.

275. Anna Strunsky Walling

Born 21 March 1877 Babinots (Babibvich), Russia (now part of Belarus)

Died 25 February 1964 New York

Peace Advocate

Socialist

Writer

Anna was influenced after witnessing a young man shot in a restaurant when he refused to sing, "God Save the Czar."

Her family emigrated to New York, so her brother could avoid serving in the Russian army.

She was a life-long socialist and belonged to groups supporting her beliefs:

- American League to Abolish Capital Punishment
- League for Industrial Democracy
- National Association for the Advancement of Colored People
- War Resisters League and the Women's Peace Party.

She met Jack London when she was a Stanford University student. They collaborated on writing a novel.

Returning to Russia in 1906, she became a correspondent for a revolutionary journal and later married the wealthy owner, William English Walling. Together they covered the 1908 Springfield Race Riot. They separated after they disagreed on U.S. World War I participation.

Her novel, *Violette of Père Lachaise*, was published in 1915.

She died before she finished her book on the Russian Revolution.

Her papers are at Yale University.

276. Martha Beatrice Webb

Born 22 January 1858 Gloucestershire, England
Died 30 April 1943 Liphook, England

Economist
Socialist
Labor historian

The term, "collective bargaining," commonly used today, was coined by Webb, a prominent voice for the co-operative and other social movements.

Her attitudes were a combination of equality with a woman's traditional knowledge of household duties.

A four-year relationship with a cabinet minister ended with his rejection of her need for independence.

She lost two sisters tragically: suicide and an overdose.

Her 1892 marriage to Sidney Webb was a successful "partnership" of agreed goals.

Her inheritance of £1000 pounds a year gave her the freedom to pursue her causes.

She believed strongly in co-operatives, writing *The Cooperative Movement in Great Britain,* although she felt worker co-operatives had weaknesses.

SPORTS

For years women were considered too delicate to participate in sports. Some might have played a round of golf or knocked a tennis ball over a net, but strenuous sports, like mountain climbing, were not considered within their abilities. When women play team sports their average earnings are about 80% of a man; this hasn't really changed from since 2003, according to the United States Bureau of Labor Statistics.

277. Senda Berenson Abbott
Born 19 March 1868 Butrimonys, Vilna Governorate, Russian Empire
Died 16 February 1954 Santa Barbara, California

Sportswoman

Gymnastics changed Russian-born Abbott from a sickly child to a proponent of physical education. She disliked the description of women in her youth as delicate and small-brained.

When her family moved to Massachusetts, they enrolled her in Boston Normal School for Gymnastics to build her strength. She was almost not admitted because of her health.

She had been more interested in the arts but had to drop out of another arts-centered program because she lacked the ability to even sit at the piano for a long time. The first months were hard, but she didn't give up.

She was so successful that she was sent to Andover to teach gymnastics.

When she arrived at Smith College, she had to sell the idea of girls' physical education. She was persuasive and arranged basketball games between classes, which won over faculty and students.

As an adult she became known as the Mother of Woman's Basketball. When she was working at Smith College, she modified the sport one year after the sport's invention.

278. Jill Kinmont Boothe

Born 16 February 1936 Los Angeles, California
Died 9 February 2012 Carson City, Nevada of a heart attack

Alpine Skier
Artist
Educator

Imagine having your photo on the cover of the 13 January 1955 *Sports Illustrated*, then a few days later having a horrendous accident and being paralyzed from the shoulders down. At 18 Boothe, an Alpine skier and national champion, had a fantastic career ahead of her until she hit a tree, breaking several vertebrae.

The injuries lasted for the rest of her life.

Eventually she regained limited use of her hands. She began painting and exhibited her work. She typed, wrote and drove.

She earned a degree in English and German at UCLA but was denied a teaching certificate, being told she was unemployable. Washington University granted her the certificate and she taught for many years as a special education teacher.

Two boyfriends were killed: one in a plane crash, one in an avalanche. She married John G. Boothe. They were still married at the time of her death.

No matter what was thrown at her, she went on to make a full life for herself.

279. Emma Rowena Gatewood (Grandma Gatewood)
Born 25 October1887 Guyan Township, Ohio
Died 4 June 1973 Gallipolis, Ohio

Ultra-light hiking pioneer

Gatewood's life on a farm had been difficult between raising 11 children and domestic abuse.

Her major accomplishment was being the first solo woman hiker who did the 2,168-mile (3,489 km) Appalachian Trail.

Then in 1955, when she was 67, she did the trail for a third time, not only the first woman, but the first person to do so.

She did not limit herself to the Appalachian Trail but also completed the Oregon Trail of 2,000 miles (3,200 km).

Raised in a poor family, she shared a bed with three siblings. Her schooling ended at eighth grade, but she read about wildlife and the Greek classics.

At 66, having discovered the Appalachian Trail in the *National Geographic*, she decided to try it. Her first attempt failed.

Perhaps the violence of her marriage helped her survive in the woods, often eating berries and finding limited shelter.

One of her longest hikes was from Independence, Missouri to Portland, Oregon. On her arrival there was a celebration: "Grandma Gatewood Day."

280. Lucy Walker
Born 10 September 1836 Canada
Died 10 September 1916 Liverpool, England

Mountain Climber

Walker became a mountain climber accidentally after a doctor advised her that walking would help her rheumatism.

She was the first woman to climb the Matterhorn, Balmhorn, Eiger, Piz Bernina and Wetterhorn, often wearing a skirt. In total she made 98 mountain climbing expeditions.

She received criticism from people who believed a woman should be at home not out climbing mountains. Worse, she was the only woman among males, none of whom were proper guardians.

Although she was a member of the Ladies' Alpine Club, she was never allowed to join the all-male Alpine club. She served as president of the woman's club.

When asked why she never married, she answered, "I love mountains and Melchoir (Melchior Anderegg, often her guide) and Melchoir already has a wife!"

She was also said to play croquet, drink champagne and eat sponge cake.

SUFFRAGISTS

Suffrage is the right to vote in local and national elections by ballot in person, mail or by voice. Women were denied that right almost from the beginning of time. Then, country by country in the western world, women began to fight to be included in the electorate. It did not come easy. Many went to jail, but little by little, women voting has become normal. In the U.S., according to Pew Research, women have a slightly higher percentage of voting then men.

281. Carrie Chapman Catt
Born 9 January 1859 Ripon, Wisconsin
Died 9 March 1947 New Rochelle, New York of a heart attack

Bank Cashier
Dishwasher
Educator
Law clerk
Suffragist

Catt traveled thousands of miles campaigning for women's voting rights, speaking to legislators and Congress. She worked for: Women's Suffrage Alliance, the League of Women Voters, National American Woman Suffrage Association (NAWSA) and the Iowa Woman Suffrage Association.

During her lifetime she held other jobs. When her father only paid half her college costs, she earned money washing dishes.

Her college group, the Crescent Literary Society, refused to let women speak. She won a rule reversal.

George Catt, her second husband, supported her work.

With NAWSA she had to fight hard internally. "Suffrage is today the strongest reform there is in this country, but it is represented by the weakest organization." Catt organized and headed its Organization Committee. It had a $5,000 budget.

When white women questioned if black women could vote, she responded that white women were of Anglo-Saxon heritage but pointed out that the Romans looked down on the Anglo-Saxons.

282. Florence Hope Luscomb

Born 6 February 1887 Lowell, Massachusetts
Died 13 October 1985 Watertown, Massachusetts

Activist
Architect
Suffragist

Luscombe considered herself a New England Yankee. One of the first ten women to graduate from M.I.T. with a degree in architecture she became a partner in a woman-owned architectural firm but spent most of her life working for women and justice.

Her interest in women's rights began in childhood when she and her mother moved to Boston and participated in women's rights events.

During one 14-week period, she gave 200 speeches to encourage acceptance of a change in the state constitution.

A trust fund allowed her to live frugally and work for her causes. She lived in co operative housing with people of all ages throughout her life, conserving her income.

Her later work either on staff or as a volunteer was with the Boston Equal Suffrage Association for Good Government, League of Women Voters, the Women's International League for Peace and Freedom, NAACP and ACLU.

Although she ran for several offices, she only won a spot on the Boston Council in 1922.

She testified before a Massachusetts legislative on Communism during the McCarthy era.

283. Alva Erskine Belmont (Vanderbilt)
Born 17 January 1853 Mobile, Alabama
Died 26 January1933 Paris, France of bronchial and heart problems

Suffragist

Alva Belmont Vanderbilt's husbands, William Vanderbilt and Oliver Belmont, were millionaires, and gave her funds to work for women's rights, including founding the Political Equality League (PEL) and the National Woman's Party. She was a member of the National American Woman Suffrage Association (NAWSA).

She wrote articles and marched in the 1912 New York Women's Vote Parade.

Against the exclusion of African Americans and immigrants in the rights groups, she encouraged leading black advocates to form a group within the PEL and invited their leaders into her private homes, but still contributed to the segregated Southern Woman Suffrage Conference.

Her political activities did not slow her building of several mansions in the U.S. and France, running balls and events typical of the super-wealthy class of her day.

One of her less admirable projects was manipulating her daughter into marrying the 9th Duke of Marlborough. The marriage was later annulled.

The pall bearers at her funeral were only women.

On "Equal Pay Day" April 12, 2016, President Barack Obama established the Belmont-Paul Women's Equality National Monument in Washington, D.C.

SURVIVORS

War, natural disasters, accidents, social upheaval, personal tragedy, it doesn't matter the cost. Women face horrendous conditions and move on. There should be a book about each of all the women who survived any of these conditions.

284. Eliza Gladys Dean aka Millvina Dean
Born 2 February 1912 Branscombe, England
Died 31 May 2009 Ashurst, England of pneumonia

Cartographer
Civil Servant
Secretary
Titanic Survivor

Only two months old when it happened, Dean does not remember surviving the sinking of the Titanic. Her father did not survive. She was eight before she learned of the catastrophe which she lived through.

The family had been in the process of moving to Wichita, Kansas, but returned to England.

During her lifetime she worked as a cartographer, civil servant and secretary.

In her 70s, she became an active Titanic survivor, attending conventions and doing interviews.

She met with her father's family members in Kansas.

Despite her participation in a documentary on the Titanic, she refused to see films and programs on the sinking of the ship.

Health and financial problems plagued her at the end of the life, and she sold many family possessions to raise funds for her needs.

285. Gisella Perl

Born 10 December 1907 Máramarossziget, Austria-Hungary (modern day Romania)
Died 16 December 1988 Herzliya, Israel

Gynecologist

Perl survived Auschwitz where she used her medical training to help women inmates despite lack of equipment and facilities. She was not deported until 1944 when Josef Mengele assigned her to work as a doctor. The abortions she performed saved the lives of many women.

Her memoir, *I was a Doctor in Auschwitz*, published in 1948, is still available.

Had he not relented, her father's objections to her medical studies would have stopped her medical studies. He feared she would "lose her faith and break away from Judaism."

After liberation, she moved to New York and attempted suicide after learning her family had been killed. She was suspected of war crimes because of her work with Mengele.

Her U.S. residency was in doubt until President Truman signed a bill allowing it. In 1951 she took her oath as a U.S. Citizen.

She became an infertility specialist at Mount Sinai Hospital.

Her last years were spent in Israel.

TATTOO ARTIST

Tattooing is said to go back to Neolithic times and crosses all cultures and all times. Otzi, also called the Iceman, whose corpse was found in 1991 in the Alps, had 61 tattoos. His mummified body is said to have lived between 3350 and 3105 BC. There are multi usages: decorative, spiritual, medical and identification tattoos. Zippla reports 25% of tattoo artists in the United States are women, out of 6,300.

286. Maud Stevens Wagner
Born 12 February 1877 Emporia, Kansas
Died 30 January1961 Lawton, Oklahoma

Circus Performer
Tattoo Artist

Wagner was working as an aerialist and contortionist when she met her future husband, Gus Wagner. She agreed to go on a date only if he would teach her tattooing.

At the time, tattoos were popular but were mostly unseen. Winston Churchill's mother had one of a snake eating its tail.

Gus taught her the "hokey-pokey" method rather than use the newly invented O'Reilly machine.

Maud Wagner was the first woman tattoo artist in America. She used her body to show off her work, which included pictures of monkeys, snakes, horses and patriotic symbols.

During the late 19th century tattooing was popular and the couple earned money travelling around the country applying their trade.

Their daughter, Lotteva, estimated her parents earned more than a bank president.

TERRORISM EXPERT

According to Wikipedia, "There is no consensus, scholarly or legal, on the definition of terrorism." Perspective plays a huge part on who is considered a terrorist. NATO wrote a report, *Gender in Terrorism and Counter-Terrorism: Data Analysis and Response.*

287. Eloise Randolph Page
Born 19 February 1920 Richmond, Virginia
Died 16 October 2002 Washington, D.C.

Central Intelligence Agency (CIA) officer

As a child, Page wanted to be a musician, but her Masters degree from George Washington University was in Political Science.

Her first job was for the British War Relief Society, a United States-based organization providing food, clothing and other essentials to the British in World War II.

Her intelligence work started in May 1942 with the Office of Strategic Services (OSS), which coordinated behind-the-lines espionage. In 1947 the OSS became the Central Intelligence Agency. At the end of the war, she continued with the CIA.

In 1978 she became the first station chief and then the first female Deputy Director of Intelligence Community. Part of her expertise was in terrorism.

In retirement, she consulted and taught at the National Defense University.

TRANSGENDER

Transgender is another of those words that is still seeking a clear definition. The simplest meaning is one whose identity differs from their gender at birth. Politically it can be a hot-button issue. Renée Richards, born Richard Raskind 19 August 19, 1934, an American ophthalmologist and tennis player, was the first transgender person in the public eye.

The World Professional Association for Transgender Health (WPATH) provides guidelines for gender-affirming care. A 2022 study was done by the *International Journal of Transgender Health*.

288. Lili Ilse Elvenes (Einar Wegener)
Born 28 December 1882 Vejle, Denmark
Died 13 September 1931 Dresden, Germany from immune failure after transplant surgery

Artist
Transgender Woman

Lili Ilse Elvesnes, the name Wegener took after transitioning, was one of the first to undergo a uterus transplant in the early 1930s. It would cost her her life. There is speculation she might have had the Klinefelter syndrome or an extra X chromosome. She was also known as Lili Elbe.

She married Gerda Gottlieb in 1904 when they were studying at the Royal Danish Academy of Fine Arts. During their marriage Elbe often dressed as a woman and pretended to be Gottlieb's sister-in-law. Her marriage was later dissolved.

Later she wanted to marry French art dealer Claude Lejeune and have children.

For her sexual reassignment surgery, she went to Hirschfeld Institute for Sexual Science. Records of the four surgeries over a two-year period were destroyed in World War II.

She was one of the first patients to have a uterus transplant and a vaginal construction.

VETERINARIANS

Of the 49,434 veterinarians currently employed in the United States 62.9% are women.

That does not differ greatly from the Canadian statistics for women veterinarians at 64.0%. Those figures are for 2023. In the United Kingdom the latest figures were for 2019, but they also reported 60%, adding that 80% of students in veterinarian schools were women.

289. Aleen Isobel Cust

Born 7 February 1868 Cordangan Manor, County Tipperary, Ireland
Died 29 January 1937 Jamaica of heart failure

Veterinarian

From childhood Cust wanted to be a vet but started medical training as a nurse at London Hospital before enrolling at William Williams's New Veterinary College in Edinburgh.

Her sex made it more difficult. Despite winning a gold medal in zoology, the college forbade her to take final exams. She was refused admission to the Royal College of Veterinary Surgeons (RCVS).

She appealed and lost. To pursue it, would have cost more than she could afford, and she didn't want to embarrass her mother, a bed chamber woman to Queen Victoria.

Her fiancé's family objected to her profession.

The RCVS refused to approve her appointment as veterinary inspector to the Galway County Council. The Council appointed her using a different title.

Cust took care of horses in World War I and joined Queen Mary's Army Auxiliary Corps. Only after the Sex Disqualification (Removal) Act 1919 was she given her diploma and allowed to practice legally in December 1922, the first woman to earn one.

WRITERS

Women have been able to write because they can put pen to paper or now fingers to keyboard without involving others. Recognition is another thing. Writers like Amantine Lucile Aurore Dupin de Francueil felt she had to take a man's name, George Sand. Women's stories are often considered less important than men's. Chick Lit and Romance have a derogatory ring. This book could have been about 300 women writers. Limiting it to these few at best was horribly difficult. Apologies to all the others.

290. Mary Anne Barker (Lady Broome, Lady Barker)
Born 29 January 1831 Spanish Town, Jamaica
Died 6 March 1911 London, England

Journalist
Writer

Mary Anne became Lady Barker when her first husband was knighted and Lady Broome when her second husband was knighted.

They moved to a New Zealand sheep station. The couple returned to England after the death of half of their sheep. Both Broomes became journalists.

After she was widowed, she married Frederick Napier.

Mary Anne became an international writer after she published *Station Life in New Zealand*, which was published in English, French and German. She published 22 books.

Her *First Lessons in the Principles of Cooking* resulted in her appointment as Lady Superintendent of the National Training School of Cooking.

She accompanied her husband to assignments in Mauritius, Australia, Barbados and Trinidad.

A Year's Housekeeping in South Africa is a vivid description of the country and culture.

She was a fierce defender of the traditional woman's domestic role, although she had left her two children from her first marriage when she went to New Zealand.

291. Minna Canth - Ulrika Wilhelmina Johnson
Born 19 March 1844 Tampere, Finland
Died 12 May 1897 Kuopio, Finland of a heart attack

Activist
Writer

Canth's play *Worker's Wife and The Pastor's Family* expressed views about woman's place in society that were contrary to those of the time.

One bishop claimed that emancipated women were against God's order.

Another play created controversy. *Hard Luck's Children* was cancelled by the Board of Trustees, silencing her radical ideas.

An adoring father had encouraged his imaginative and creative daughter to get a good education starting with a school for factory workers' children. Later she attended but did not finish the Jyväskylä Teacher Seminary, the first school offering women higher education.

Shortly before the birth of their seventh child her husband died. He had been an editor of Keski-Suomi newspaper which published her articles on women's issues, promoting controversy. The following year she wrote fiction pieces for *Päijänne,* a competing paper.

292. Elizabeth Cleghorn Gaskell
Born 29 September 1810 London, England
Died 12 November 1865 Holybourne, England

Writer

A prolific writer, she published short stories, novels and a biography of Charlotte Brontë requested by Patrick Brontë, Charlotte's father. Her work tended to eliminate the more salacious details of Victorian society.

She was one of two children of eight that survived. Her mother died when she was a toddler, and although her father sent her to live with an aunt, she had a pleasant childhood. Her education was traditional for her time in the arts, classics and manners for young women.

Although she seldom saw her father, he encouraged her education.

She married a Unitarian minister. Her first writing described her daughter Marianne's development as well as the role of motherhood.

Because she lived in Manchester, she became aware of life in an industrial city which also influenced her writing.

Travels to Belgium and Germany were to influence her writing.

At first, she self-published and later published under a pseudonym.

She achieved success with her 1848 novel *Mary Barton*, inspired by the death of her infant son.

The *Bury Times* reported her death as "Mrs. Gaskell, the authoress and biographer, was suddenly struck by death on Sunday last, while in the act of reading to her daughters."

293. Mahasweta Devi
Born 14 January 1926 Dhaka, India
Died 28 July 2016 Kolkata, India of a heart attack

Activist
Writer

Devi was born into an artistic and Brahmin family with her parents being writers and her brother a film maker.

She became a novelist producing over 100 novels.

She was also a leftist working to improve tribal rights through her careful research and direct experience living with other groups. She concentrated on peoples' struggles, especially women and marginalized Indians. She studied the people of Adivasi and Dalit.

Her passions were noted when she spoke at the 2006 Frankfurt Book Fair. Many in the audience cried.

She said she wasn't the creator of her stories: they were Indian peoples' stories.

Talking Humanities has said of her that "… her writings are an anomaly to the myth that survives within the academic scholarship. This is the myth of a separation between field and text, a debate that has drawn responses from across the disciplines."

Devi died from a major heart attack.

294. Nh Dini
Born 29 February 1936 Semarang, Central Java, Dutch Indies
Died 4 December 2018 Semarang, Central Java, Indonesia after a
car crash

Feminist
Flight Attendant
Writer

An advocate of childhood literacy, Dini was in charge of a non-profit promoting reading to youngsters.

Her love of writing began in second grade. When she was 15, she read her poems written in the Javanese alphabet on State Radio.

Her short stories delved into sexuality and women's issues.

Like many writers she worked at another job while writing. She was a flight attendant when she published short stories called *Dua Dunia (Two Worlds)*. Later, she also wrote radio plays, many with a strong feminist theme.

Despite her success, she only received royalties for some of her writing.

Because of her marriage to French Counsel Yves Coffin, from whom she was later divorced, she lived in Japan, Manila, Phnom Penh and Detroit before returning to Indonesia where she spent the last part of her life.

295. Isabelle Wilhelmine Marie Eberhardt
Born 17 February 1877 Geneva, Switzerland
Died 21 October 1904 Aïn Séfra, Algeria in a flash flood

Explorer
Journalist
Writer

Perhaps her "illegitimate" birth, a father who had been her mother's tutor, an anarchist and former priest converting to atheism, was part of her becoming a nonconformist. Her father saw that she was well educated.

She learned Arabic, French, German, Italian, Latin, Greek and Russian.

Her first short stories were published when she was a teenager.

Photographer Louis David invited her to move to Algeria.

Her conversion to Islam and her choice of dressing as a man made her an outcast in the international community. It did not help that she spent much time with Arabs.

Many thought her a spy or at least an agitator.

She drank, used drugs and considered sex as a pastime. Her behavior caused people to treat her as a man, although she was heterosexual.

She survived an assassination attempt but forgave her assassin.

Her manuscripts were first published two years after her death in a flash flood. They were well received.

296. Harriet Jane Farley
Born 18 February1812 Claremont, New Hampshire
Died 12 November 1907 New York, New York

Abolitionist
Editor of the *Lowell Offering, New England Offering*
Suffragist
Writer

Although her family was poor, and she had to contribute financially by doing piecemeal sewing, her education was sound. Her father was principal of Atkinson Academy, which claimed to be the oldest U.S. co-educational school.

She went to work in Lowell textile mills as well as writing for the *Lowell Offering*, an offshoot of a mill writing group. She was later editor of its 32-page monthly magazine. One of its goals was to show mill workers as intelligent women. Writers Charles Dickens, Anthony Trollope and George Sand spoke highly of it.

The publication about mill girls became known in England for insight into the women's lives.

At one point it became too conservative for its audience.

After moving to New York, she wrote for women's magazines.

At times, she was unpopular because she defended factory management.

She took a two-decade writing hiatus to raise her husband's four children.

297. Ida A. Husted Harper

Born 18 February 1851 Fairfield Township, Indiana
Died 14 March 1931 Washington, D.C. of a cerebral hemorrhage

Educator
Journalist
Suffragist
Writer

Harper's first wrote for newspapers in Terre Haute, Indiana under a man's name. For 13 years she wrote *A Woman's Thoughts*. Her topics were varied but she always believed that a woman had "the right to pursue whatever vocation in life she is best adapted for …"

Her husband, lawyer Thomas Winans Harper, legal counsel for a railroad union founded by Eugene V. Debs, disapproved of his wife's work. They were eventually divorced.

Debs invited Harper to edit *The Woman's Department*, a monthly column in *Locomotive Firemen's Magazine*.

The Harpers had one child. Like her mother, Winnifred H. Cooley became a writer and journalist. When her daughter went to school in Indianapolis and California, Harper followed her.

Harper's major work was a three-volume biography of Susan B. Anthony, a friend through the National American Woman Suffrage Association. Anthony asked Harper to write the biography.

In 1989 she became managing editor of the *Daily News*, one of the first women in that role on a political daily.

298. Irmgard Keun
Born 6 February 1913 Charlottenburg, Prussia
Died 5 May 1982 Cologne, Germany

Writer

A fake suicide, pseudonyms, living in France and the Netherlands and a lawsuit are some ways Keun survived Nazi Germany.

Her well-off family had given her more freedom to explore than many women of her time and place had.

Gilgi, her first book about an ambitious, determined and fearless, woman, was successful. Once her books were banned, things became difficult. Her attempts to join an official author's association were denied.

She claimed she divorced her husband because he was a Nazi sympathizer but continued communicating with him.

She used pseudonyms for her writing despite the bans. During the war years she used an alias in the Netherlands. When she returned to Nazi Germany, she created a false suicide report.

Her alcoholism caused commitment to the Bonn State Hospital psychiatric ward for five years.

Her books are representative of the 1930s and show the complexities of male-female relationships.

299. Lucy Larcom
Born 5 March 1892 Beverly, Massachusetts
Died 17 April 1893 Boston, Massachusetts

Bobbin Girl
Bookkeeper
Educator
Poet
Writer

Her experiences were as varied as factory work and poet.

She co-founded *Rushlight Literary Magazine*, a submission-based student literary magazine.

From 1865 to 1873, she edited the Boston-based *Our Young Folks*, which merged with *St. Nicholas Magazine* in 1874.

In 1889, Larcom published one of the best-known accounts of New England childhood, *A New England Girlhood*, commonly used as a reference in studying antebellum American childhood. The autobiographical text covers the early years of her life in Beverly Farms and Lowell where she worked in the mills in a variety of roles from bobbin girl to bookkeeper. She wrote for a co-operative magazine created by mill women.

Her poems appeared in places like *The Atlantic*.

After moving to Illinois, she taught school. Returning to Massachusetts she taught also at the Wheaton and Monticello Female Seminaries. At one point she earned $40 for three months teaching.

300. Catherine Lucille Moore

Born 24 January 1911 Indianapolis, Indiana
Died 4 April 1987 Hollywood, California

Science fiction writer

Moore was a sickly child who spent her time reading science fiction and fantasy. She became one of four women to write science fiction and fantasy, opening the genre to other women writers.

When she married Henry Kuttner, another science fictionist, they collaborated until his death in 1958. She had a certain style: he was a cerebral storyteller.

Her first publication was three short stories at Indiana University.

She chose her pen name C.L. Moore for other publications to keep her employer from knowing their secretary was working on the side.

Her *Shambleau* earned $100. Her stories appeared in 10+ science fiction magazines.

After her husband's death she taught at the Southern California University. She wrote television scripts for popular programs such as *Maverick* and *77 Sunset Strip*.

When she married Thomas Reggie, she stopped writing.

The Science Fiction Writers of America nominated her as the first woman to be Grand Master of the Genre. Because she suffered from Alzheimer's, Reggie asked it to be withdrawn.

This section groups women who worked in many different areas. The number of women who successfully made a contribution to more than on field is important. Many were wives and mothers are the same time. They are listed alphabetically and the numbers refer to the section where readers can find their biographies.

ABOLITIONISTS

Lydia Maria Child 1, Harriet Jane Farley 296, Lucretia Coffin Mott 2, Clarina Irene Howard Nichols 3, Sarah Parker Remond 4, Ernestine Louise Polowsky Rose 25, Maria W. Stewart 5, Laura Matilda Towne 110

ACADEMICS/SCHOLARS

Ada Sara Adler 6, Nora Kershaw Chadwick 7, Gertrude Mary Hirst 8, Janet Lembke 9

ACTIVISTS

Khadijah Muhammad Abdullah Al-Jahami 147, Sadie Tanner Mossel Alexander 9, Louie Bennett 148, Georgina Beyer 216, Zitkala-Sa (Red Bird) Simmons Bonnin 27, Nannie Helen Burroughs 94, Mary Ann Camberton Shadd Cary 167, Lydia Leyah (Leah) Chase 11, Lydia Maria Child 1, Septima Poinsette Clark 96, Marvel Jackson Cooke 149, Mahasweta Devi 293, Mary Williams Dewson 233, Crystal Catherine Eastman 12, Marie Equi 184, Natalya Khusainovna Estemirova 150, Heloise Ruth First 248, Berta Isabel Caceras Flores 13, Matilda Joslyn Gage 234, Nancy Green 14, Vilma Lucila Espín Guilloisn 249, Dorothy Irene Height 15, Maria Julia Hernandez 16, Jane Jacobs 17, Minna Canth-Ulrika Wilhelmina Johnson 291, Florynce Rae Kennedy 18, Gauri Lankesh 151, Muna Lee 19, Viola Fauver Liuzzo 20, Florence Hope Luscomb 282, Lucretia Coffin Mott 2, Sarojini Naidu 21, Mary White Ovington 22, Annie Mae Aquash Pitou 24, Conception Arnel Ponte 23, Sarah Parker Remond 4, Alice Mary Robertson

224, Ernestine Louise Polowsky Rose 25, Augusta Christine Fells Savage 45, Maria W. Stewart 5, Doris Gwendolyn Tate 26, Madam C.J. Walker (Sarah Breedlove) 79, Anna Strunsky Walling 275, Margaret Bush Wilson 168, Evelyn M. Witkin 267

ACTRESS
Florynce Rae Kennedy 18, Jean Muir (Fullarton) 28, Elizabeth J. Magie Phillips 146

ADVENTURER/EXPLORER
Isabelle Wilhelmine Marie Eberhardt 295, Ella Maillart 153

AGRONOMIST
Vivica Aina Fanny Bandler 123

ANTHROPOLOGISTS
Zora Neale Hurston 30

ARCHEOLOGISTS/PALEONTOLOGISTS
Elizabeth Grayson Hartley FSA 31, Mary Douglas Leakey 32, Lady Hester Lucy Stanhope 33, Lucy Myers Wright Mitchell 130, Gertrude Caton Thompson 34

ARCHITECTS
Florence Hope Luscomb 282, Julia Morgan 35, Norma Merrick Sklarek 36, Hilda Taba 107, Gertrud Taeuber-Arp 49

ARTISTS
Gillian Ayres 37, Maria Martin Bachman 38, Jill Kinmont Boothe 278, Dorothea Frances Canfield 95, Ruth Windmüller Duckworth 39, Elisabeth Louise Vigée Le Brun 40, Constance Georgine Booth Markievicz 253, Shirley Ardell Mason 41, Maria Sibylla Merian 42, Elizabeth Catlett Mora 43, Rachel Ruysch 44, Augusta Christine

Fells Savage 45, Miriam Schapiro 46, Amrita Sher-Gil 47, Elisabetta Sirani 48, Sophie Henriette Gertrud Taeuber-Arp 49, Lili Ilse Elvenes (Einar Wegener) 288

ASTRONOMERS

Williamina Fleming 50, Caroline Lucretia Herschel 51, Margaretha (Maria) Kirch 52, Henrietta Leavitt 53, Nicole-Reine Lepaute 54, Vera Florence Cooper Rubin 55, Mary Somerville 177, Beatrice Muriel Hill Tinsley 56

ATHLETES

Bertha Eckstein-Diener 126, Annie Cohen Kopchovsky 57, Marie Marvingt 58, Hazel McCallion 221

ATOMIC BOMB VICTIM

Sadako Sasaki 59

AUDITOR

Anne Scheiber 105

AVIATION

Florence Lowe "Pancho" Barnes 60, Sophie Blanchard 61, Georgia Ann "Tiny"Thompson Broadwick 62, Bessie Coleman 63, Nh Dinim 294, Sabiha Gökçen 64, Joy Bright Hancock 199, Ida Holdgreve 268, Joy Lofthouse 65, Marie Marvingt 58, Betty Ann Ong 66, Marina Lavrentievna Popovich 67, Irina Fyodorovna Sebrova 68

BAD ASS WOMEN

Anne Bonny 69, Leonarda Cianciulli 70, Nexhmije Hoxha 71, Fanny Efimovna Kaplan (Feiga Haimovna) 250, Catherine Monvoisin 72, Grace O'Malley 73, Gertrud Emma Scholtz-Klink (Maria Stuckbrock) 74, Valerie Jean Solanas 75, Agnes Waterhouse 75, Aileen Carol Wuornos 77

BALLOONIST
Marie Marvingt 58, Sophie Blanchard 61

BUSINESSWOMEN
Mary Elizabeth Anderson 139, Amalie Auguste Melitta Bentz 141, Helen Bates "Penny" Chenery 78, Caresse Crosby 143, Mary Fields 172, Mary Somerville 177, Ruth Graves Wakefield 82, Madam C.J. Walker (Sarah Breedlove) 79

CALLIGRAPHER
Elizabeth Lucar 17

CARTOGRAPHER
Eliza Gladys Dean 284

CHEFS/COOKS
Pancha Carrasco 195, Leyah (Leah) Chase 11, Nancy Green 14, Marella Hazan 80, Marjorie Child Husted 81, Ruth Graves Wakefield 82

CHEMIST
Ruth Mary Rogan Benerito 140

CHILDREN'S ADVOCATE
Bertha Marian Holt 83

CLOCKMAKER
Nicole-Reine Lepaute 54

COMMUNIST
Marta Matamoros 158

CONSERVATIONIST
Dian Fossey 84

COMPUTING EXPERTS
Anita Borg 85, Grace Brewster Hopper 86, Augusta Ada King 87, Arfa Abdul Karim Randhawa 88

COSMOLOGIST
Beatrice Muriel Hill Tinsley 56

CRIMINOLOGIST
Frances Glessner Lee 89

CRITIC
Margarita Miller-Verghy 101

DANCER
Ayu Bulantrisna Djelantaik 90, Gertrud Taeuber-Arp 49

DIETICIAN
Ruth Graves Wakefield 82

DIPLOMAT
Alexandra Mikhailovna Kollontai 220, Alva Myrdal 102

DRAG QUEEN
Georgina Beyer 216

ECONOMISTS
Edith Abbott 93, Sadie Tanner Mossel Alexander 91, Emily Greene Balch 92, Joy Bright Hancock 199, Grace Raymond Hebard 129, Martha Beatrice Webb 93

EDITOR

Lilias Eveline Armstrong 170, Emily Greene Balch 92, Matilda Joslyn Gage 234, Harriet Jane Farley 296, Joy Bright Hancock 199

EDUCATORS/PROFESSORS/TEACHERS

Edith Abbott 93, Lilias Eveline Armstrong 170, Gillian Ayres 37, Emily Greene Balch 92, Pura Teresa Belpré y Nogueras 169, Zitkala-Sa (Red Bird) Simmons Bonnin 27, Jill Kinmont Boothe 278, Nannie Helen Burroughs 94, Clary Campoamor Rodriguez 166, Dorothea Frances Canfield 95, Carrie Chapman Catt 281, Septima Poinsette Clark 96, Haydée Santamaría Cuadrado 245, Crystal Catherine Eastman 12, Gertrude "Trudy" Belle Elion 261, Natalya Khusainovna Estemirova 150, Sarah Fuller 97, Vilma Lucila Espín Guilloisn 249, Keiko Fukuda 173, Mary Agnes Hallaren 198, Ida A. Husted Harper 297, Grace Raymond Hebard 129, Nora Herlihy 98, Alice Marie Jourdain Hildebrand 237, Zora Neale Hurston 30, Harriet Jacobs 271, Sophia Louisa Jex-Blake 187, Lucy Larcom 299, Muna Lee 19, Mary Mason Lyon 99, Charlotte Maria Shaw Mason 100, Elizabeth Catlett Mora 43, Jean Muir (Fullarton) 28, Alva Myrdal 102, Florence Nwanzuruahu Nkiru Nwapa 103, Maureen O'Carroll 222, Kalliroe Parren 122, Savitribai Phule 104, Alice Mary Robertson 224, Mary Jane Safford-Blake 188, Mary Ann Camberton Shadd Cary 167, Anne Scheiber 105, Eve Kosofsky Sedgwick 106, Norma Merrick Sklarek 36, Maria Emilie Snethlage 266, Hilda Taba 107, Clotilde Tambroni 108, Martha Carey Thomas 109, Laura Matilda Towne 110, la Cara Deloria Anpetu Waste Win (Beautiful Day Woman) 29, Margarita Miller-Verghy 101, Emma Hart Willard 111

ENGINEER

Yvonne Madelaine Brill 112, Edith Clarke 113, Grace Raymond Hebard 129, Elizabeth Muriel Gregory "Elsie" MacGill 115, Julia

Morgan 35, Marina Lavrentievna Popovich 67, Virginia Tower Norwood 116, Elizabeth J. Magie Phillips 146, Wanda Rutkiewicz 206, Beatrice Shilling 117

ENVIRONMENTALISTS
Blanca Jeannette Kawas Fernández 118, Judith Arundell Wright 119

ETHNOGRAPHER
Ila Cara Deloria Anpetu Waste Win (Beautiful Day Woman) 29

FACTORY WORKER
Georgia Ann "Tiny" Thompson Broadwick 62, Kitty Harris 135, Lucy Larcom 299, Adelheid Dworschak Popps 274

FARMER
Clarina Irene Howard Nichols 3, Muna Lee 19, Ruth Sager 253

FEMINISTS
Nannie Helen Burroughs 94, Clary Campoamor Rodriguez 166, Nh Dinim 294, Mary Williams Dewson 233, Crystal Catherine Eastman 12, Marie Equi 184, Vilma Lucila Espín Guilloisn 249, Shulamith Bath Shmuel Ben Ari Firestone 120, Kate Campbell Hurd-Mead 185, Sophiea Louisa Jex-Blake 187, Muna Lee 19, Linda Nochlin 131, Conception Arnel Ponte, Kalliroe Parren 122, Adelheid Dworschak Popps 274, Ernestine Louise Polowsky Rose 25, Miriam Schapiro 46, Vale Emma Anne Paterson 159, Margarita Miller-Verghy 101, Etta Lubina Johanna Palm d'Aelders 132, Elizabeth J. Magie Phillips 146, Huda Sha'arawi or Hoda Sha'rawi 121, Valerie Jean Solanas 75

FILM / THEATER DIRECTORS
Vivica Aina Fanny Bandler 123, Zora Neale Hurston 30, Larissa Shepitko 124

GAME DESIGNER
Danielle "Dan" Bunten Berry 227

GEOGRAPHER
Ellen Churchill Semple 125

HERETIC
Jeanne-Marie de La Motte-Guyon 236

HISTORIANS
Edith Abbott, Bertha Eckstein-Diener 126, Lucy Myers Wright Mitchell 130, Linda Nochlin 131, Ragnhild Hatton 128, Grace Raymond Hebard 129, Martha Beatrice Webb 276

HOME ECONOMIST
Marjorie Child Husted 81

INTELLIGENCE OFFICERS / SPIES
Inayat Khan aka Nora Baker 133, Cecile Pearl Witherington Cornioley 242, Virginia Hall Goillot 134, Vilma Lucila Espín Guilloisn 249, Jeanette Guyot 240, Kitty Harris 135, Etta Lubina Johanna Palm d'Aelders 132, Gabrielle Maria Petit 136, Agnes Smedley 137, Diana Ruth Wellesley 138

INVENTORS
Mary Elizabeth Anderson 139, Ruth Mary Rogan Benerito 140, 141. Amalie Auguste Melitta Bentz 141, Marie-Anne Victoire Gillain Boivin 190, Yvonne Madelaine Brill 112, Georgia Ann "Tiny" Thompson Broadwick 62, Edith Clarke 113, Josephine Cochrane 142, Caresse Crosby 143, Beulah Louise Henry 144, Margaret Eloise Knight. 145, Elizabeth J. Magie Phillips 146,

JOURNALISTS
Khadijah Muhammad Abdullah Al-Jahami 147, Mary Anne Barker 290, Louie Bennett 148, Clary Campoamor Rodriguez 166, Lydia Maria Child 1, Marvel Jackson Cooke 149, Crystal Catherine Eatman 12, Isabelle Wilhelmine Marie Eberhardt 295, Bertha Eckstein-Diener 126, Natalya Khusainovna Estemirova 150, Heloise Ruth First 248, Marina Ginestà i Coloma 273, Ida A. Husted Harper 297, Gauri Lankesh 151, Camille Lepage 152, Ella Maillart 153, Marie Marvingt 58, Margarita Miller-Verghy 101, Clarina Irene Howard Nichols 3, Mary White Ovington 22, Kalliroe Parren 122, Elizabeth J. Magie Phillips 146, Conception Arnel Ponte 22, Adelheid Dworschak Popps 274, Agnes Smedley 137, Hazel Freeman Smith 156

JUDGE
Edith Hahn Beer 161, Martha Wright Griffiths 219

LABOR LEADERS
Florence Lowe "Pancho" Barnes 60, Louie Bennett 148, Margrith Bigler-Eggenberger 163, Jean Muir (Fullarton) 28, Agnes Nestor 157, Marta Matamoros 158, Emma Anne Paterson 159, Crystal Lee Sutton 160

LAWYERS
Edith Hahn Beer 161, Marianne Beth 162, Bigler-Eggenberger 163, Mary Ann Camberton Shadd Cary 167, Carrie Chapman Catt (law clerk) 281, Margrith Crystal Catherine Eastman 12, Bettisia Gozzadini 164, Martha Wright Griffiths 219, Grace Raymond Hebard 129, Lidia Poët 165, Conception Arnel Ponte 22, Clary Campoamor Rodriguez 166, Anne Scheiber 105, Margaret Bush Wilson 168

LECTURER/SPEAKER
Matilda Joslyn Gage 234, Margrith Bigler-Eggenberger 163, Florynce Rae Kennedy 18, Annie Cohen Kopchovsky 57, Sarah Parker Remond 4, Ruth Graves Wakefield 82

LIBRARIAN
Pura Teresa Belpré y Nogueras 169

LINGUIST/TRANSLATOR
Lilias Eveline Armstrong 170, Zitkala-Sa (Red Bird) Simmons Bonnin 27, Clary Campoamor Rodriguez 166, Bertha Eckstein-Diener 126, Janet Lembke 9, Muna Lee 19, Kató Lomb171, Ana Pauker 223, Clotilde Tambroni 108, Martha Carey Thomas 109, Ila Cara Deloria Anpetu Waste Win (Beautiful Day Woman) 29

LOBBYIST
Clarina Irene Howard Nichols 3

LOCKSMITH
Irina Fyodorovna Sebrova 68

MAID/DOMESTIC WORKER
Zora Neale Hurston 30, Adelheid Dworschak Popps 274

MAIL CARRIER/POSTAL WORKER
Mary Fields 172, Alice Mary Robertson 224

MARTIAL ARTS
Keiko Fukuda 173

MATHEMATICIANS
Marie-Sophie Germain 174, Grace Brewster Hopper 85, Mary Winston Jackson 114, Augusta Ada King 87, Nicole-Reine Lepaute

54, Elizabeth Lucar 175, Amalie Emmy Noether 176, Mary Somerville 177

MEDICAL DOCTORS
Safiye Ali 178, Ana Aslan 258, Kate Waller Barrett 179, Tewhida Ben Sheikh 180, Elizabeth Blackwell 181, Yelena Georgievna Bonner 10. Angélique Marguerite Le Boursier du Coudray 191, Rebecca Lee Crumpler 182, Marie Josefina Durocher 183, Marie Equi 184, Kate Campbell Hurd-Mead 185, Aletta Henriëtte Jacobs 186, Sophiea Louisa Jex-Blake 187, Kathleen Florence Lynn 201, Gisella Perl 285, Mary Jane Safford-Blake 188, Clara Emilia Smitt-Dryselius 189

MIDWIVES
Marie Josefina Durocher 183, Marie-Anne Victoire Gillain Boivin 190, Mary Carson Breckinridge 192, Marie-Louise Lachapelle 193

MILITARY
Lilian Bader 194, María Josefa Gabriela Cariño de Silang 203, Pancha Carrasco 195, Susan Ahn Cuddy 196, Crystal Catherine Eastman (anti-military) 12, Florence Beatrice Green 197, Mary Agnes Hallaren 198, Joy Bright Hancock 199, Sheila Anne Hellstrom 200, Marina Lavrentievna Popovich 67, Mary Anne Talbot (John Taylor) 204, Ecaterina Teodoroiu 205

MOUNTAINEER
Bertha Eckstein-Diener 126, Wanda Rutkiewicz 206, Lucy Walker 280

MOTHER OF LOST GENERATION
Caresse Crosby 143

MUSICIAN
Elizabeth Lucar 175, Zitkala-Sa (Red Bird) Simmons Bonnin 27

NANNY
Crystal Catherine Eastman 12, Nancy Green 14, Vivian Dorothy Maier 213, Maria Petit 136

NATURALIST
Janet Lembke 9, Maria Sibylla Merian 42, Sha'arawi or Hoda Sha'rawi 121

NURSES
Khadijah Muhammad Abdullah Al-Jahami 147, Mary Carson Breckinridge 192, Rebecca Lee Crumpler 182, Sister Elizabeth Kenny 207, Marie Marvingt 58, Irena Stanisława Sendler 241, Baroness Eva Charlotta Lovisa Sofia (Sophie) Mannerheim 208, Gladys Skillett 209, Ecaterina Teodoroiu 205

PACIFIST
Emily Greene Balch 92, Kathleen Lonsdale 264, Anna Strunsky Walling 275

PARACHUTISTS
Georgia Ann "Tiny" Thompson Broadwick 62

PATHOLOGISTS
Sophia Getzowa 210, Alessandra Giliani 211

PHILANTHROPIST
Madam C.J. Walker (Sarah Breedlove) 79

PHILOLOGIST
Nora Kershaw Chadwick 7, Clotilde Tambroni 108

PHOTOGRAPHERS
Imogen Cunningham 212, Sophia Getzowa 210, Vivian Dorothy

Maier 213, Ella Maillart 153, Georgette Louise Meyer (Dickey Chapelle) 155, Lucia Moholy (Lucy Shultz) 214

PIRATE
Anne Bonny 69, Grace O'Malley "Grainne Ni Mhaille" 73

POET
Lil Milagro de la Esperanza Ramírez Huezo Córdoba 244, Lucy Larcom 299, Muna Lee 19, Sarojini Naidu 21, Savitribai Phule 104, Clotilde Tambroni 108, Judith Arundell Wright 119

PHILOSOPHER
Marie-Sophie Germain 174, Alice Miller 230, Mary Somerville 177

PHYSICIST
Virginia Tower Norwood 116

POLITICIANS
Georgina Beyer 216, **Anita Lee Blair** 217, Hattie Ophelia Watt Caraway 218, Martha Wright Griffiths 219, Mikhailovna Kollontai 220, Constance Georgine Booth Markievicz 253, Alexandra Hazel McCallion 221, Alva Myrdal 102, Sarojini Naidu 21, Maureen O'Carroll 222, Ana Pauker 223, Adelheid Dworschak Popps 274, Alice Mary Robertson 224, Clary Campoamor Rodriguez 166, Gertrud Emma Scholtz-Klink 225

PRINTMAKER
Gillian Ayres 37

PUBLISHER
Clary Campoamor Rodriguez 166. Caresse Crosby 143, Mary Ann Camberton Shadd Cary 167, Hazel Freeman Smith 156

PRISONER
Mimi Reinhardt 226, Gladys Skillett 209

PROGRAMMER
Danielle "Dan" Bunten Berry 227

PROSTITUTE
Aileen Carol Wuornos 77

PSYCHOLOGISTS
Lou Andreas-Salomé 228, Marie Louise von Franz 229, Alice Miller 230

PUBLISHER
Florence Nwanzuruahu Nkiru Nwapa 103

RACER
Beatrice Shilling 117

RANCHER
Mary Elizabeth Anderson 139

REFORMERS
Elisabeth Achelis 232, Kate Waller Barrett 179, Mary Williams Dewson 233, Nora Herlihy 98, Kathleen Lonsdale 264, Charlotte Maria Shaw Mason 100, Lucretia Coffin Mott 2, Savitribai Phule 104

RELIGIOUS LEADERS
Agnes of Bohemia 235, Nannie Helen Burroughs 94, Alice Marie Jourdain Hildebrand 237, Jeanne-Marie de La Motte-Guyon 236, Marguerite Porete 238, Susanna Wesley 239

RESISTANCE FIGHTERS
Cecile Pearl Witherington Cornioley 242, Jeanette Guyot 240, Irena Stanisława Sendler 241

RESTAURANT
Catherine Breshkovsky 243, Florence Lowe "Pancho" Barnes 60

REVOLUTIONARIES
Lil Milagro de la Esperanza Ramírez Huezo Córdoba 244, Haydée Santamaría Cuadrado 245, Mairéad Farrell 246, Vera Nikolayevna Figner Filippova 247, Heloise Ruth First 248, Vilma Lucila Espín Guillois 249, Fanny Efimovna Kaplan (Feiga Haimovna) 250, Musine Kokalari 251, Sybil (or Sibbell) Ludington 252, Constance Georgine Booth Markievicz 253, Alexandra Mikhailovna Kollontai 220, Marie-Jeanne 'Manon' Roland de la Platière 254, Pritilata Waddedar 255

SAILOR
Mary Ann Brown Patten 256

SALESWOMAN
Gabrielle Maria Petit 136

SCIENTISTS
Marian Ewurama Addy 257, Ana Aslan 258, Alice Augusta Ball 259, Alice Eastwood Josephine Ettel Kablick 263, Alice Eastwood 260, Gertrude "Trudy" Belle Elion 261, Sophia Getzowa 210, Eloise "Elo" R. Giblett 262, Kathleen Lonsdale 264, Ruth Sager 253, Mary Somerville 177, Maria Emilie Snethlage 266, Evelyn M. Witkin 267

SEAMSTRESSES/NEEDLEWORK/MILLINER
Esther Steinberg Gluck 269, Kitty Harris 135, Ida Holdgreve 268, Fanny Efimovna Kaplan (Feiga Haimovna) 250, Elizabeth Lucar

175, Marta Matamoros 158, Adelheid Dworschak Popps 274, Clary Campoamor Rodriguez 166

SECRETARIES
Cecile Pearl Witherington Cornioley 242, Eliza Gladys Dean aka Millvina Dean 284, Gertrude "Trudy" Belle Elion 261, Hermine "Miep" Gies 270, Elizabeth J. Magie Phillips 146, Ruth Sager 265

SERIAL KILLER
Leonarda Cianciulli 70, Aileen Carol Wuornos 77

SHOEMAKER
Marta Matamoros 158

SLAVES
Nancy Green 14, Harriet Jacobs 271, Bethany Veney 272

SOCIAL WORKER
Alice Mary Robertson 224

SOCIALISTS
Emily Greene Balch 92, Catherine Breshkovsky 243, Marina Ginestà i Coloma 273, Crystal Catherine Eastman 12, Alva Myrdal 102, Mary White Ovington 22, Adelheid Dworschak Popps 274, Anna Strunsky Walling 275, Martha Beatrice Webb 276

SONGWRITER
Khadijah Muhammad Abdullah Al-Jahami 147

SPORTS
Senda Berenson Abbott 277, Jill Kinmont Boothe 278, Emma Rowena Gatewood (Grandma Gatewood) 279

SUFFRAGISTS
Louie Bennett 148, Carrie Chapman Catt 281, Matilda Joslyn Gage 234, Harriet Jane Farley 296, Ida A. Husted Harper 297, Grace Raymond Hebard 129, Aletta Henriëtte Jacobs 186, Florence Hope Luscomb 282, Constance Georgine Booth Markievicz 253, Yevonde Philone Middleton 215, Mary White Ovington 22, Ernestine Louise Polowsky Rose 25, Mary Jane Safford-Blake 188, Martha Carey Thomas 109, Alva Erskine Belmont (Vanderbilt) 283

SURVIVORS
Edith Hahn Beer 161, Eliza Gladys Dean aka Millvina Dean 284

TATTOO ARTIST
Maud Stevens Wagner 286

TERRORISM EXPERT
Eloise Randolph Page 287

TRANSGENDER
Lili Ilse Elvenes (Einar Wegener) 288

VETERINARIANS
Aleen Isobel Cust 289

VITICULTURIST
Mary Elizabeth Anderson 139

WRITERS
Edith Abbott 93, Khadijah Muhammad Abdullah Al-Jahami 147, Lou Andreas-Salomé 228, Lilias Eveline Armstrong 170, Inayat Khan aka Nora Baker 133, Mary Anne Barker 290, Louie Bennett 148, Nannie Helen Burroughs 94, Zitkala-Sa (Red Bird) Simmons Bonnin 27, Clary Campoamor Rodriguez 166, Dorothea Frances Canfield 95, Minna Canth - Ulrika Wilhelmina Johnson 291, Lydia

About the Author

D-L Nelson is a Swiss/Canadian writer who grew up in New England. The author of 17 books, she has worked as a journalist and in corporate communications. She now lives in the South of France and Switzerland with her "boys," her husband, aviation journalist Rick Adams, and her dog Sherlock. Visit her website at www.dlnelsonwriter.com and her blog http://theexpatwriter.blogspot.com

www.ingramcontent.com/pod-product-compliance
Lightning Source LLC
Jackson TN
JSHW021126080725
87299JS00003B/12